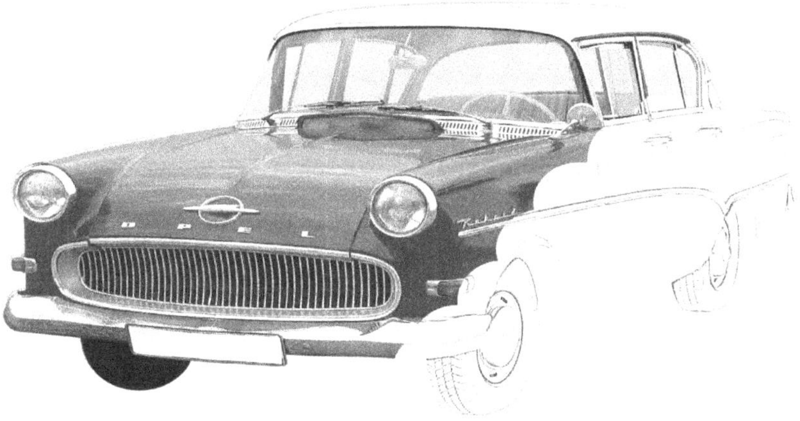


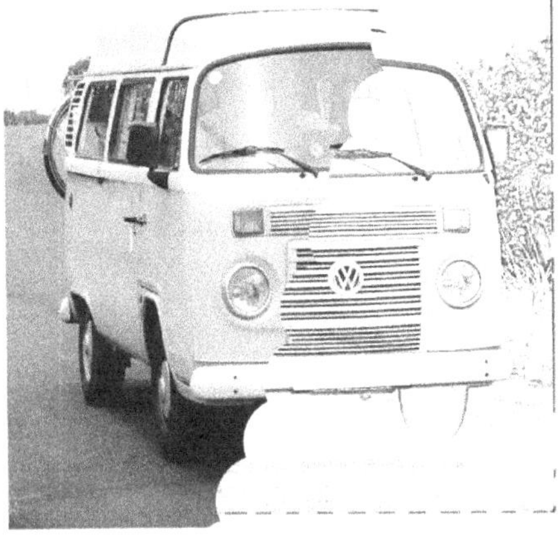

# Classic Cars

## Adult Coloring Book

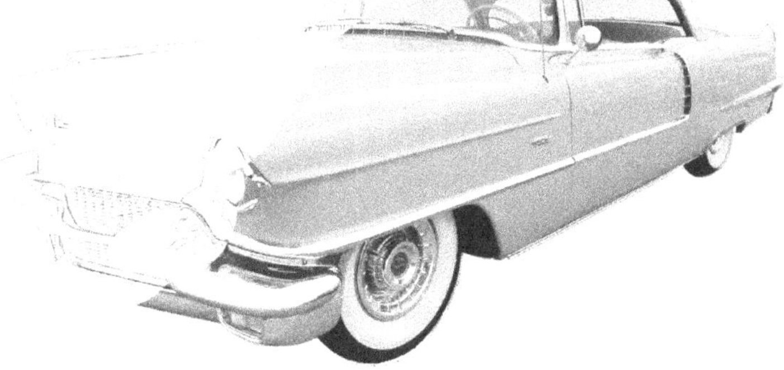

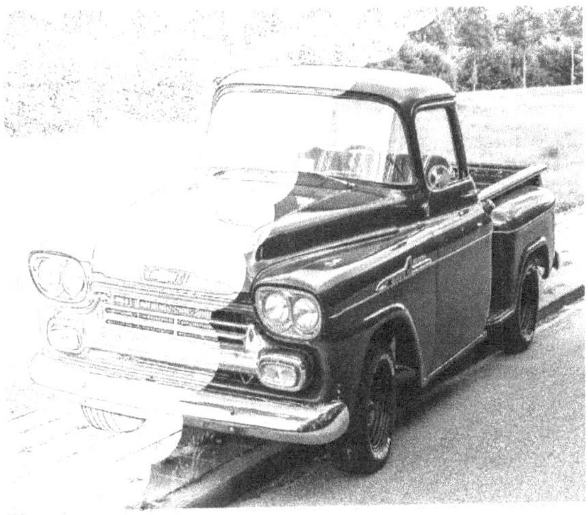

ISBN-13: 978-1983589225
ISBN-10: 1983589225

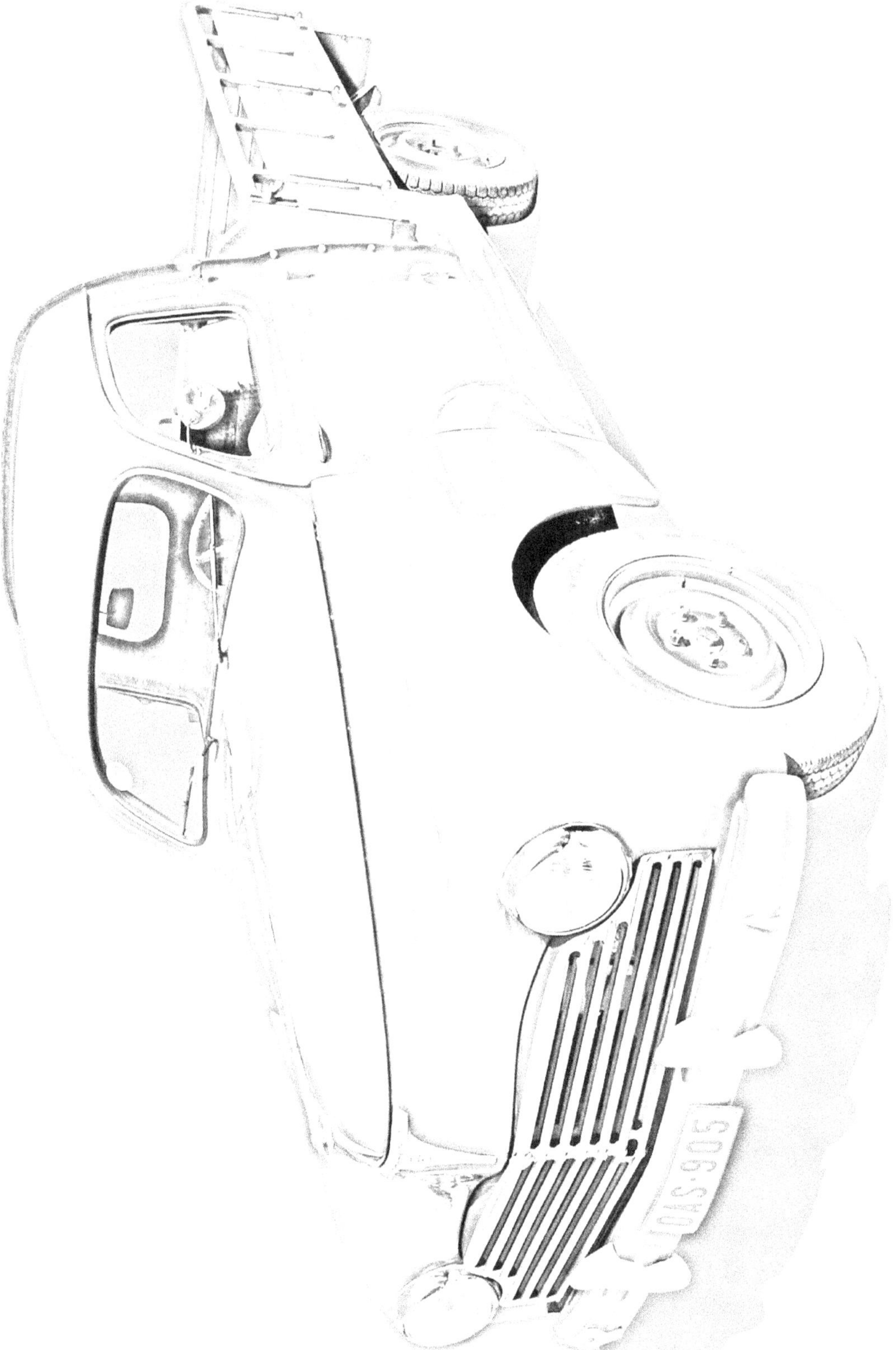

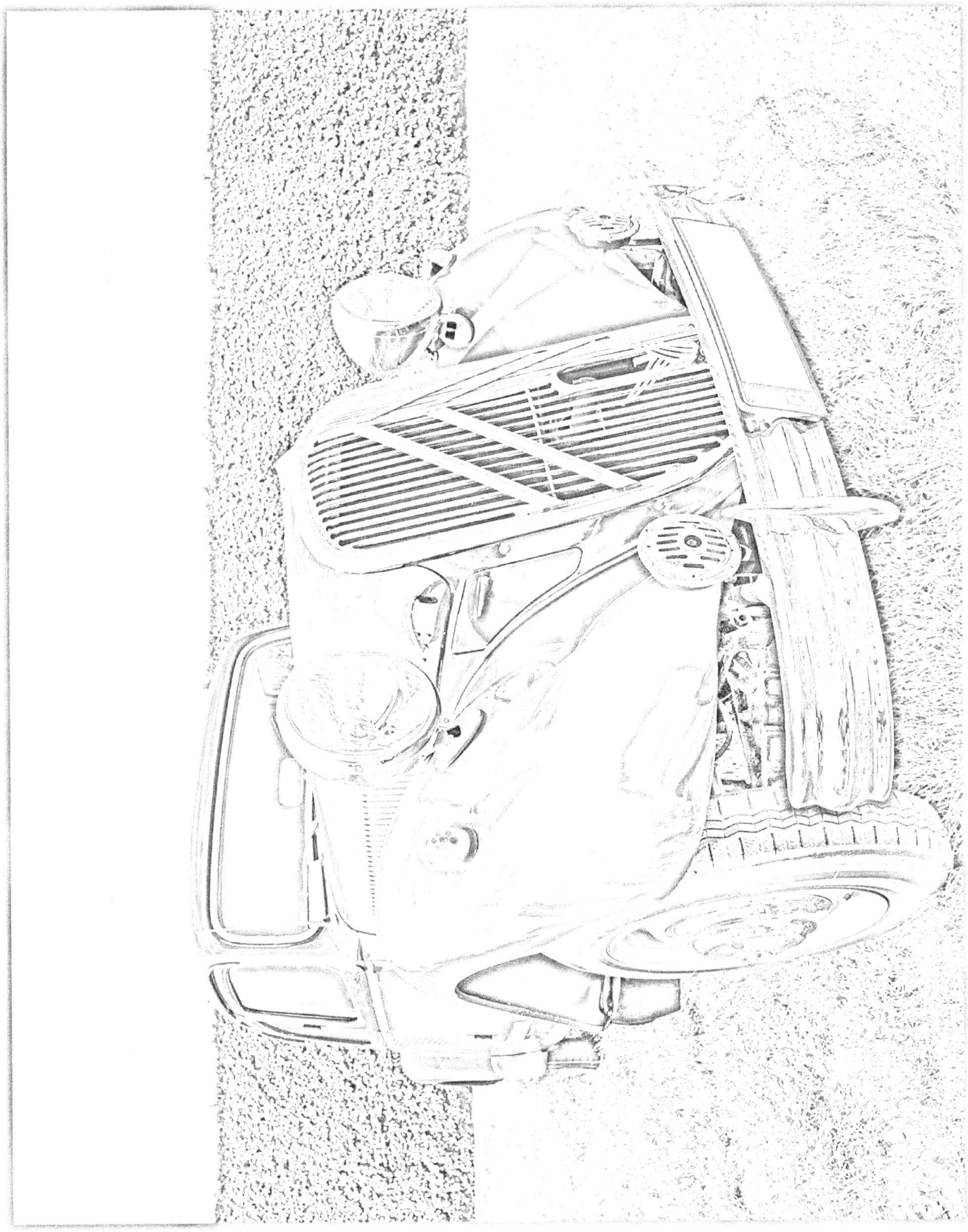

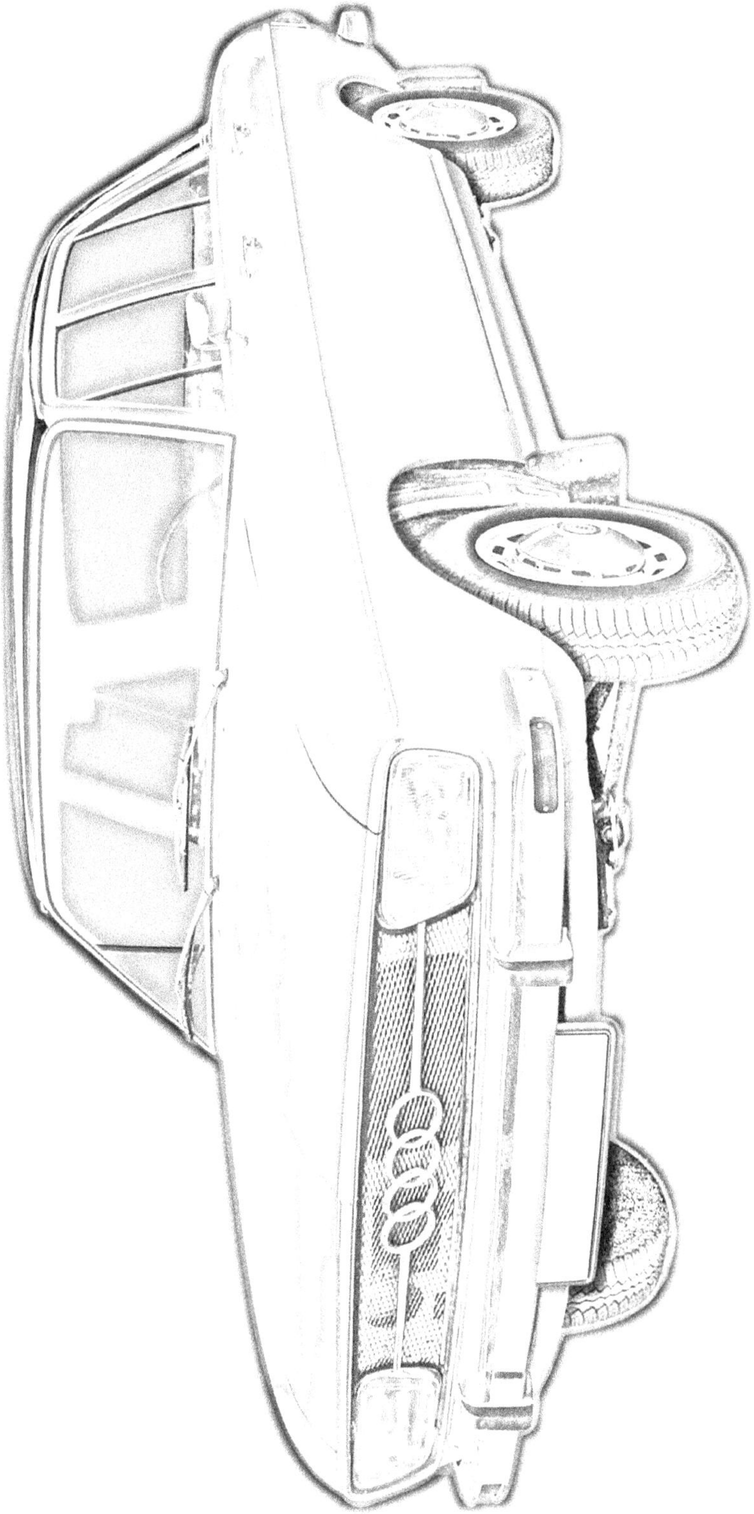

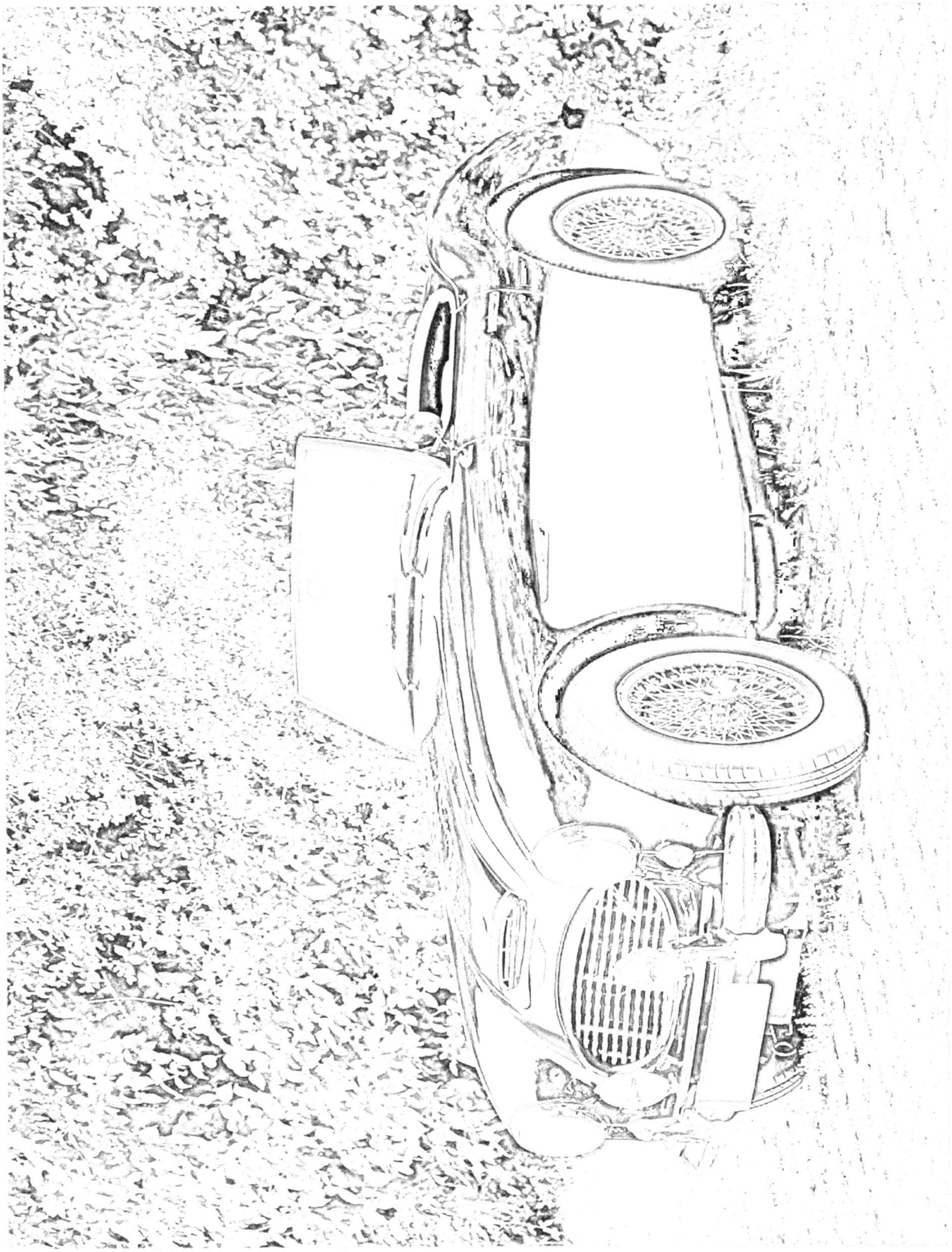

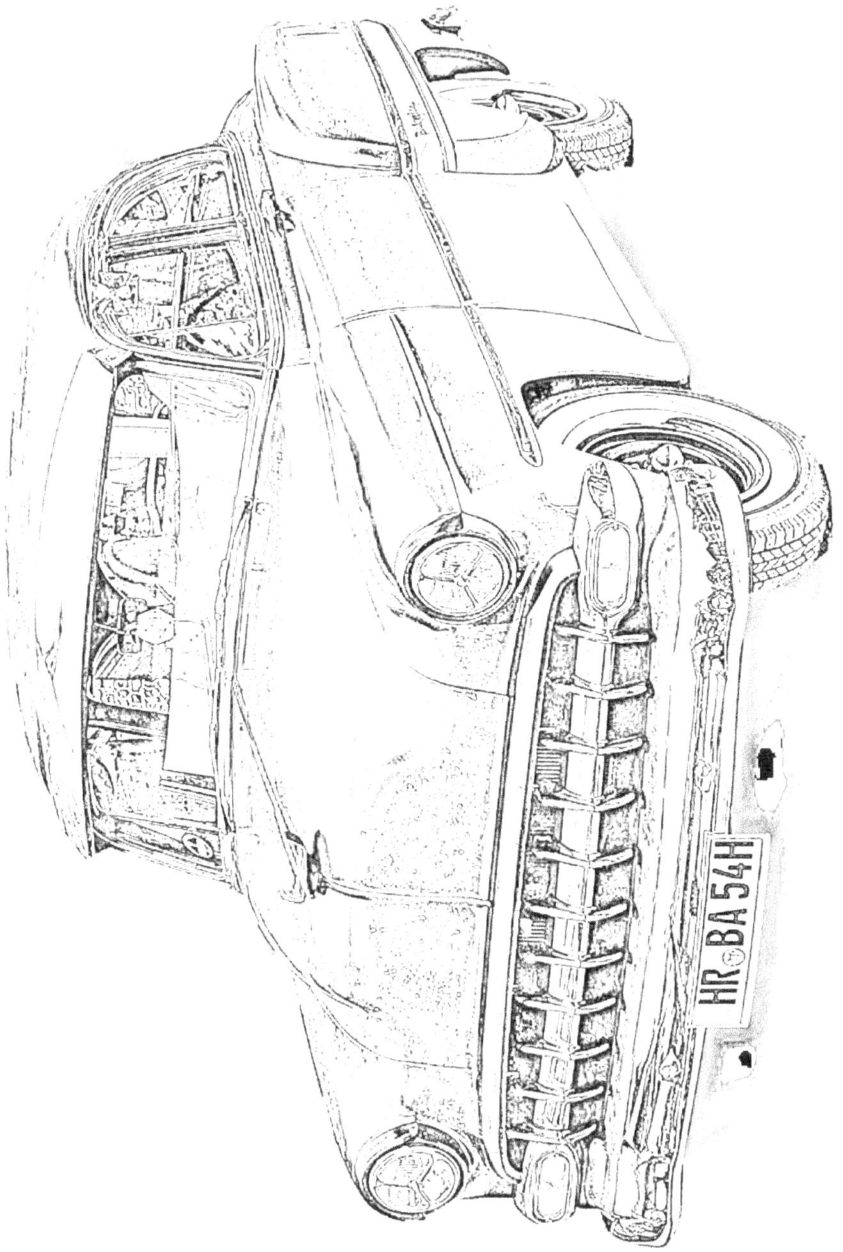
HR BA 54H

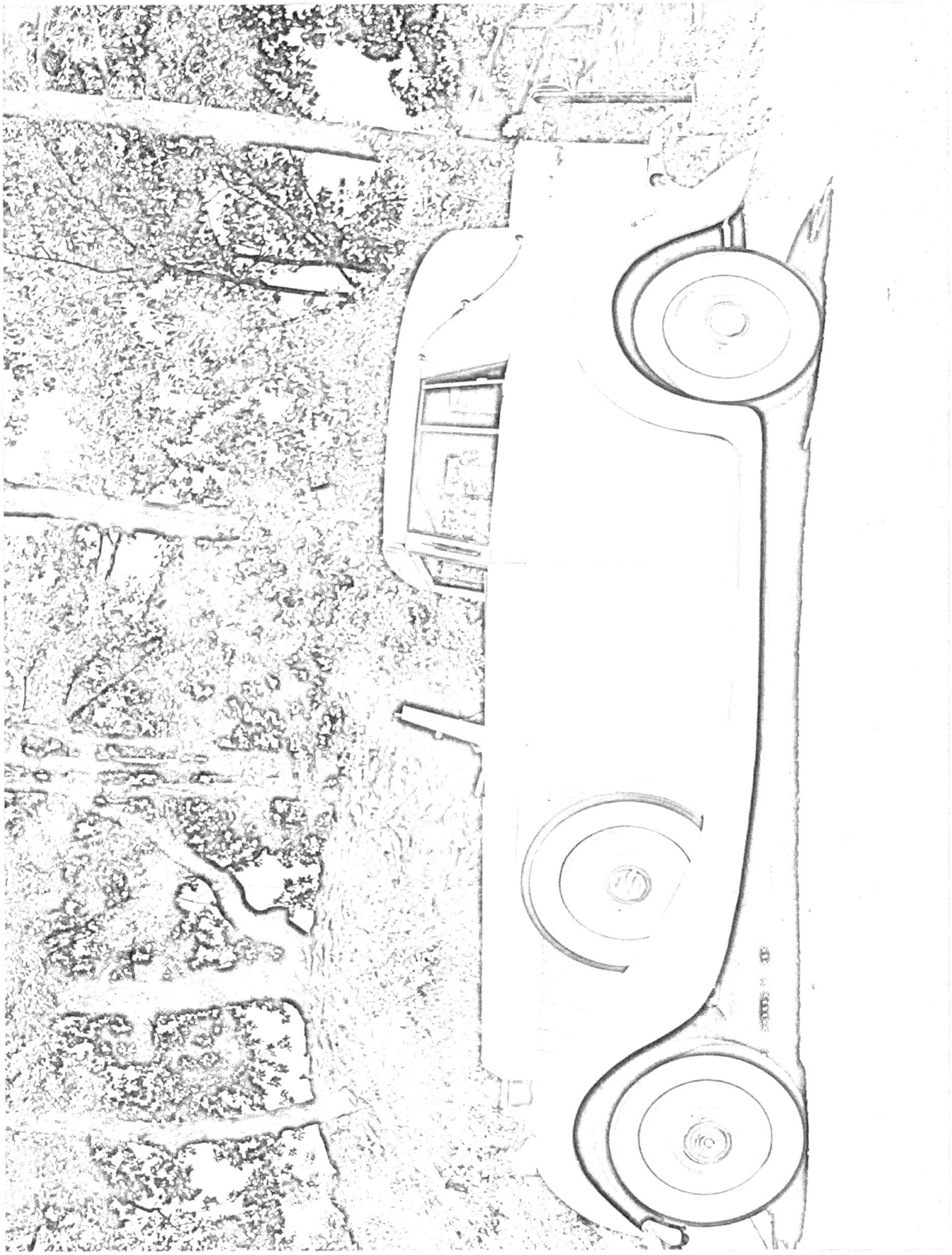

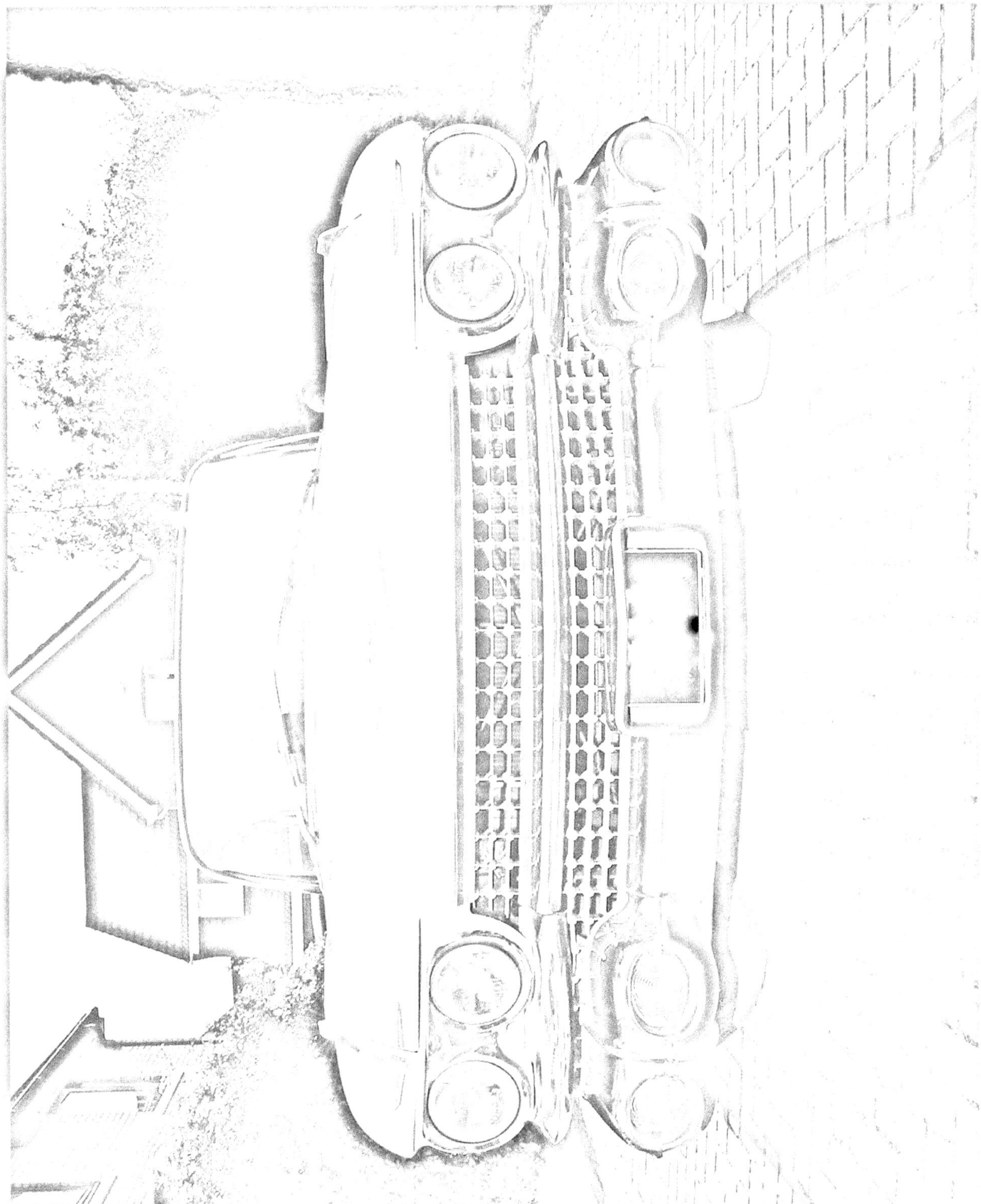

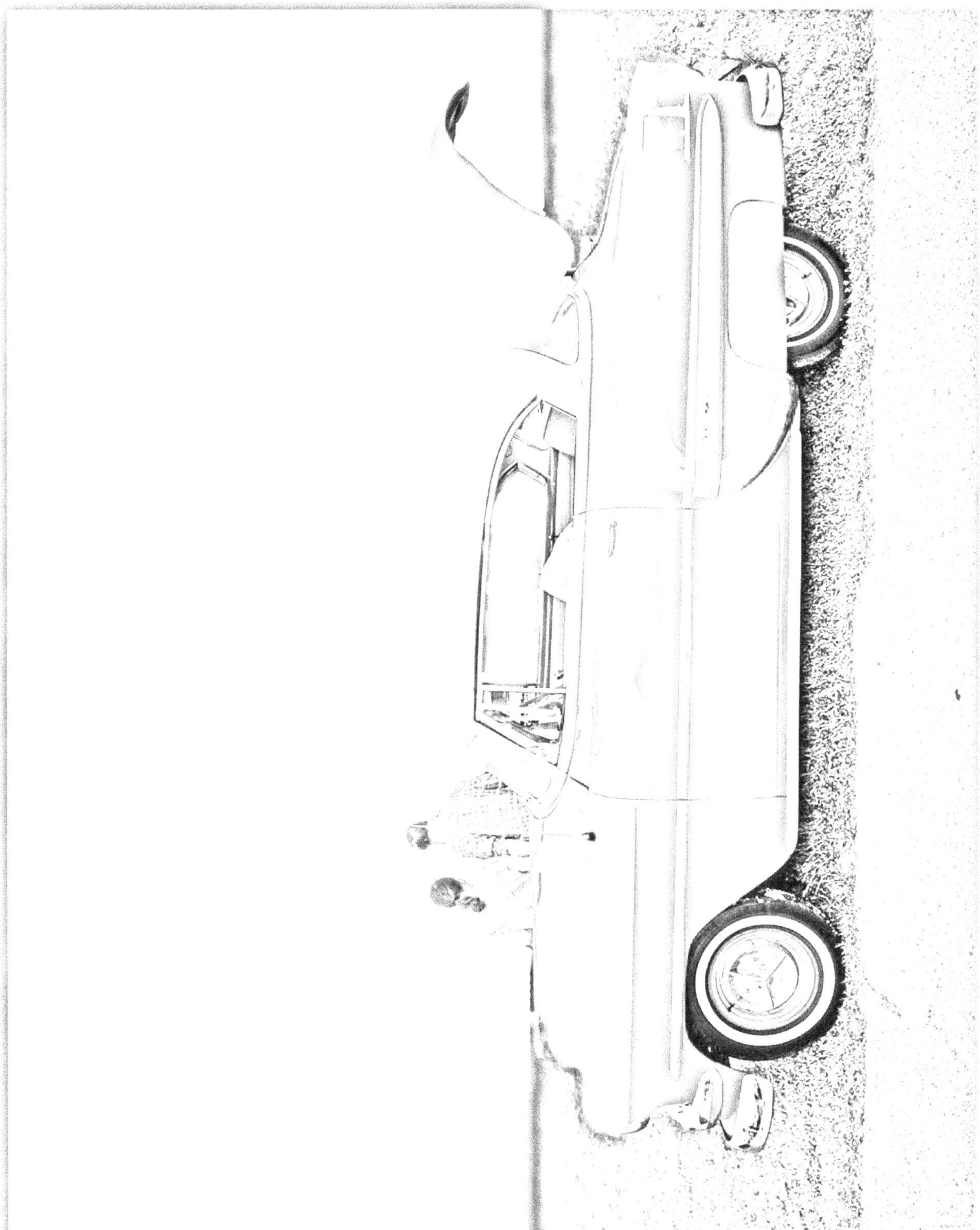

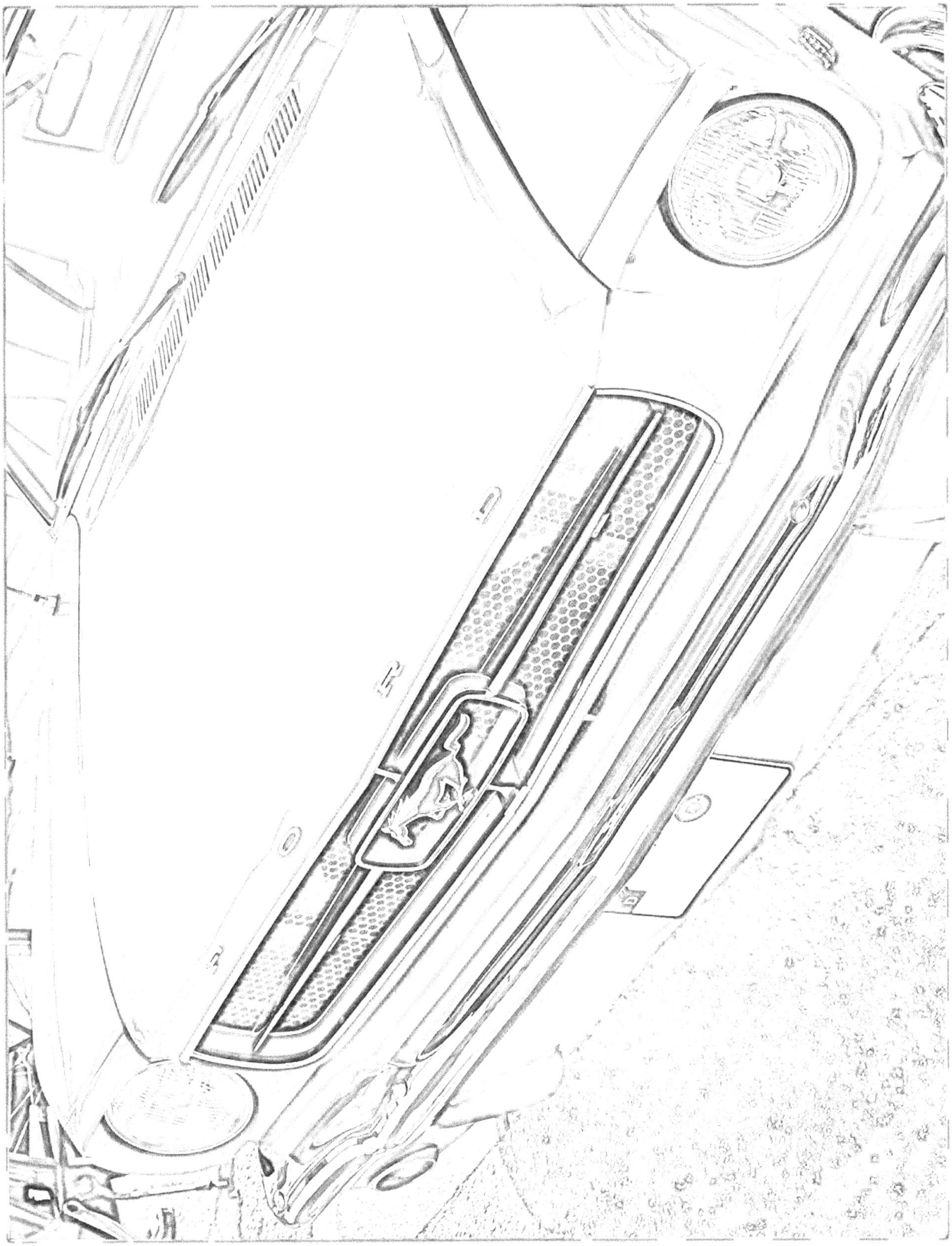

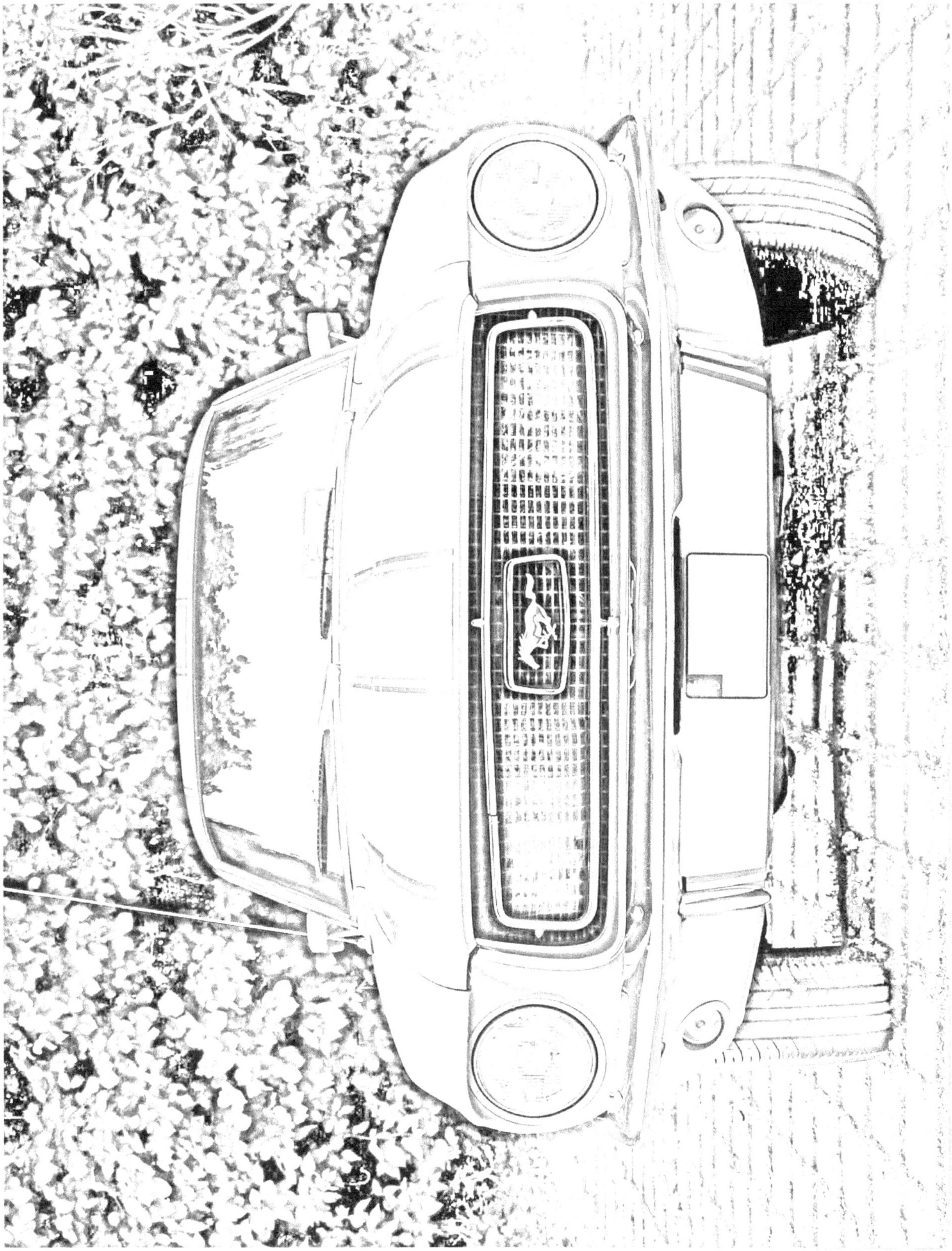

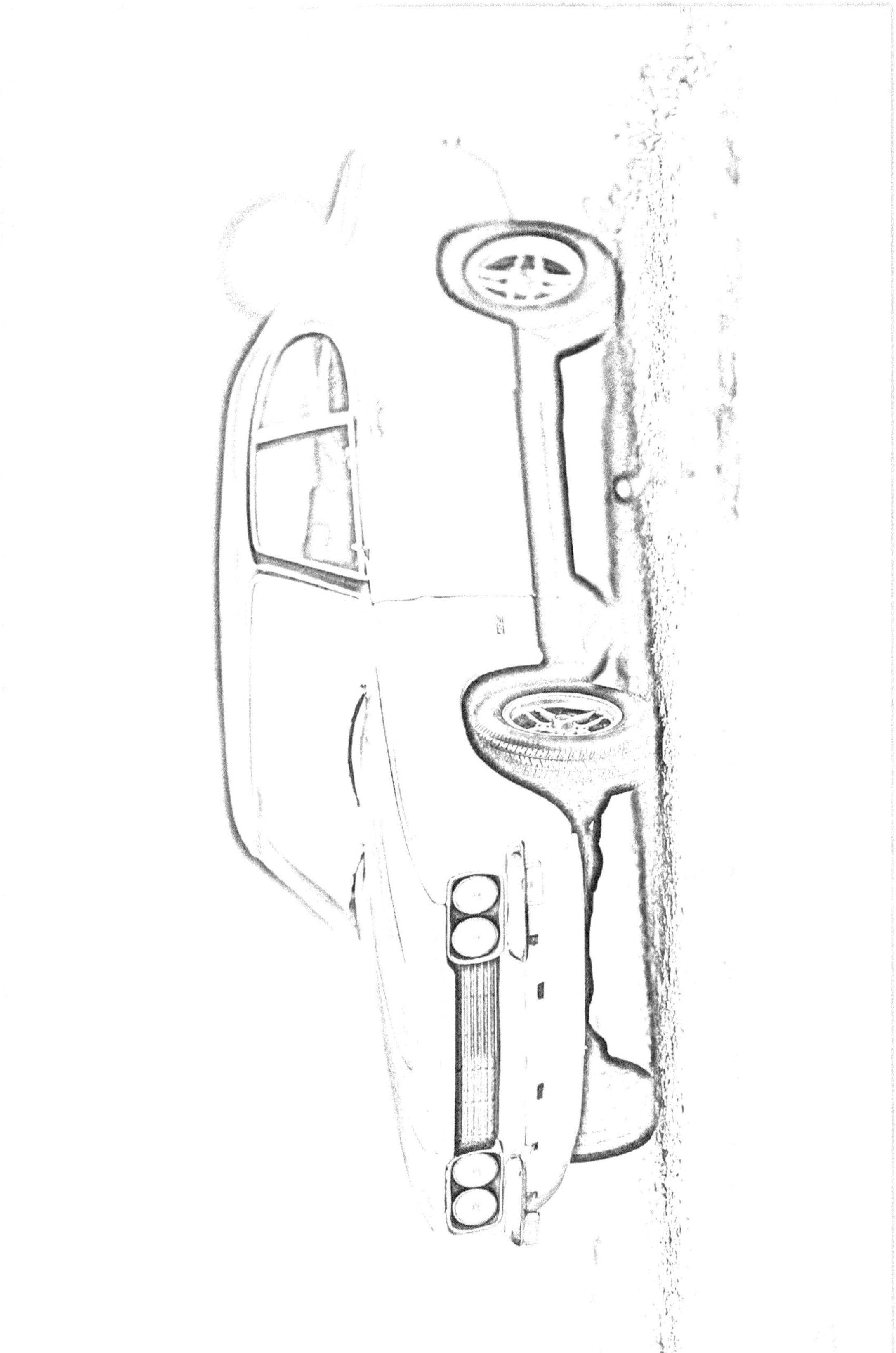

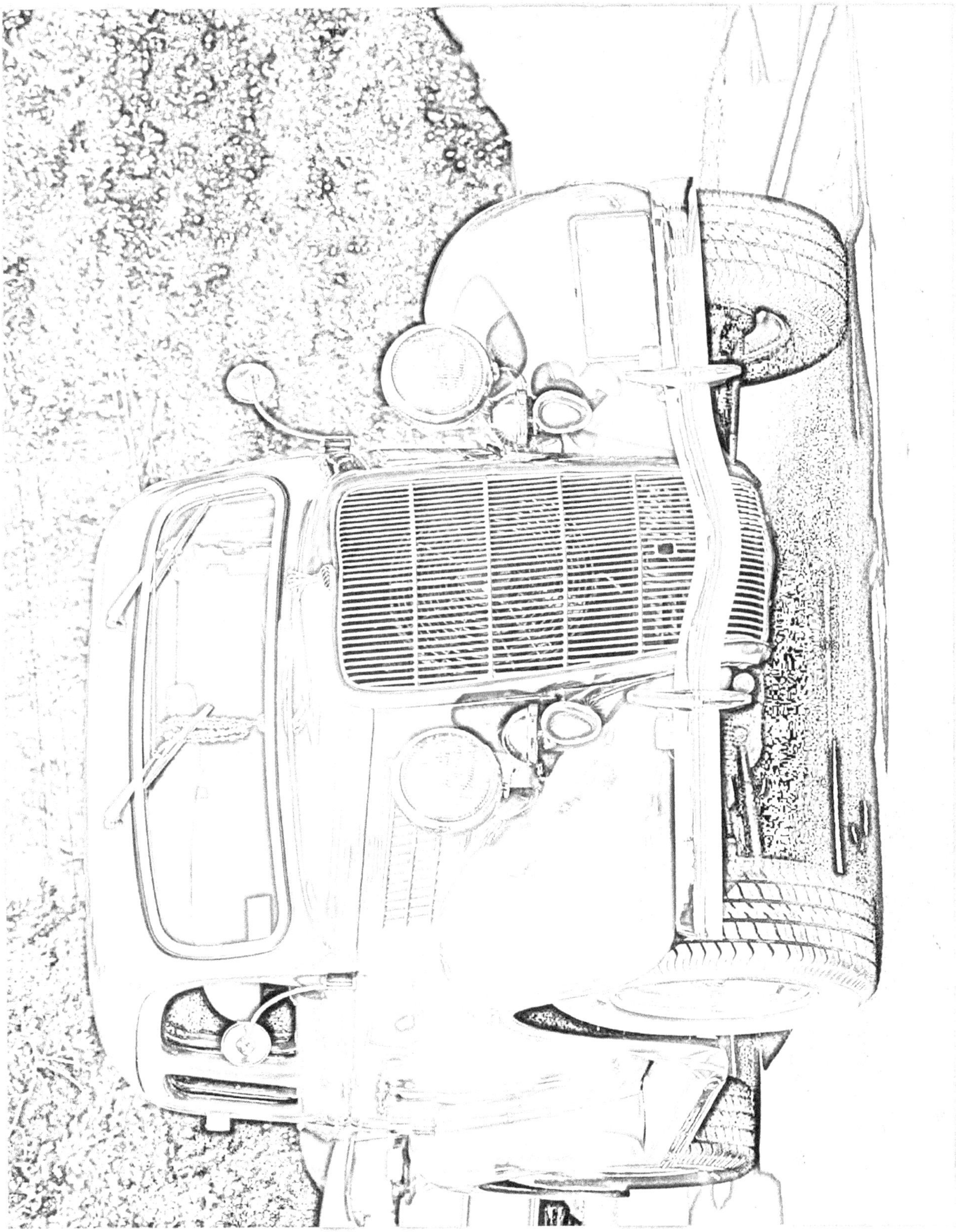

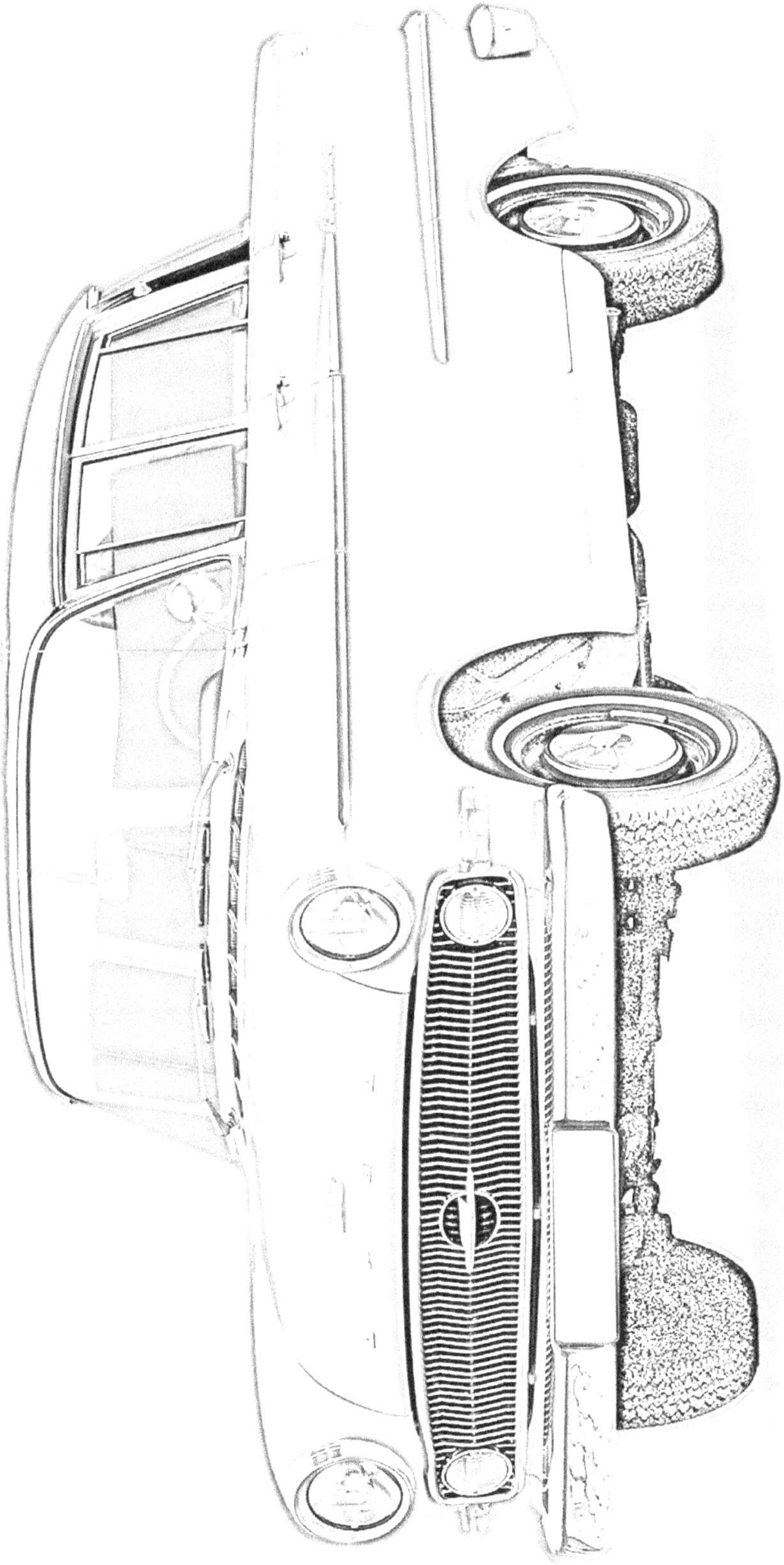

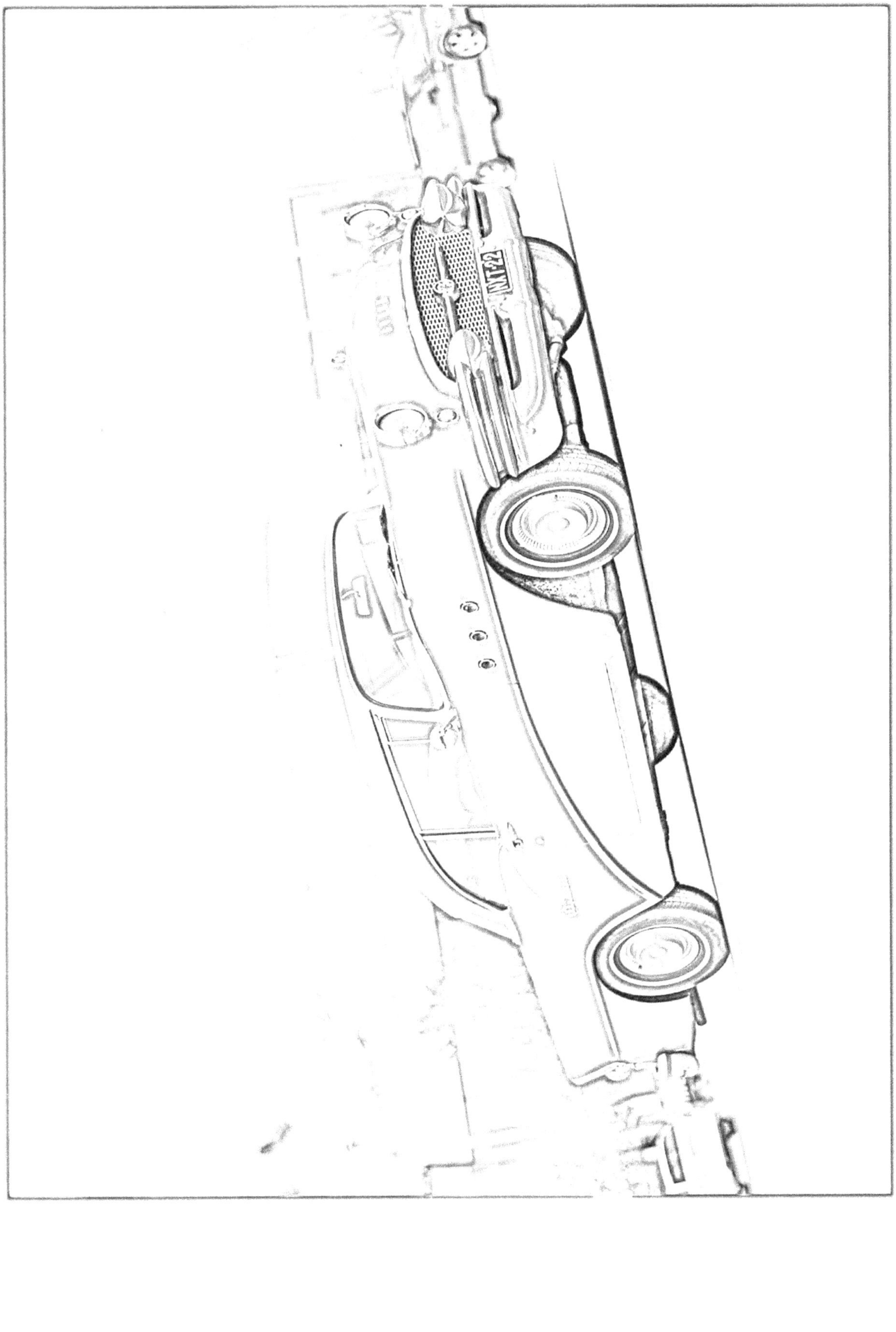

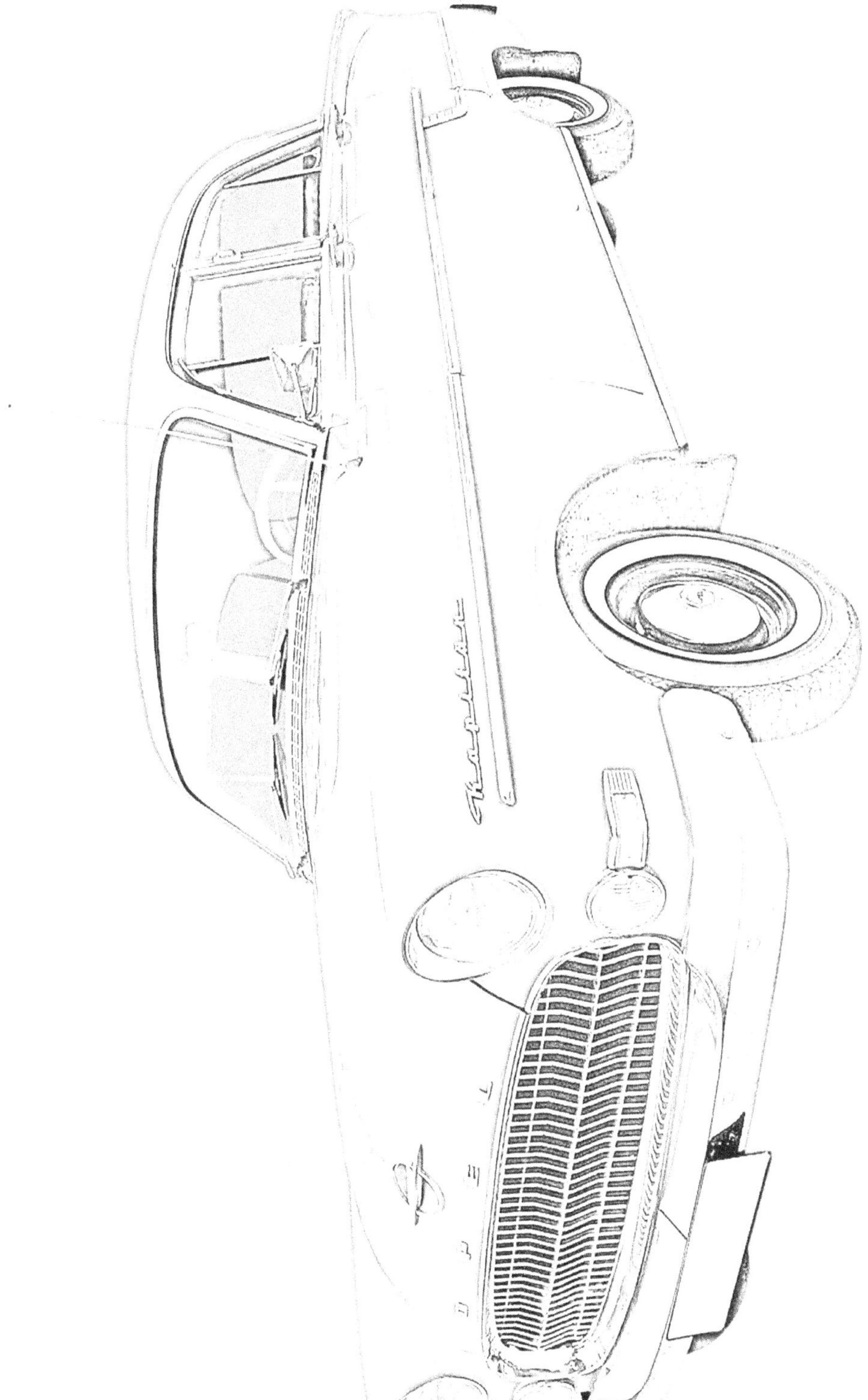
OPEL

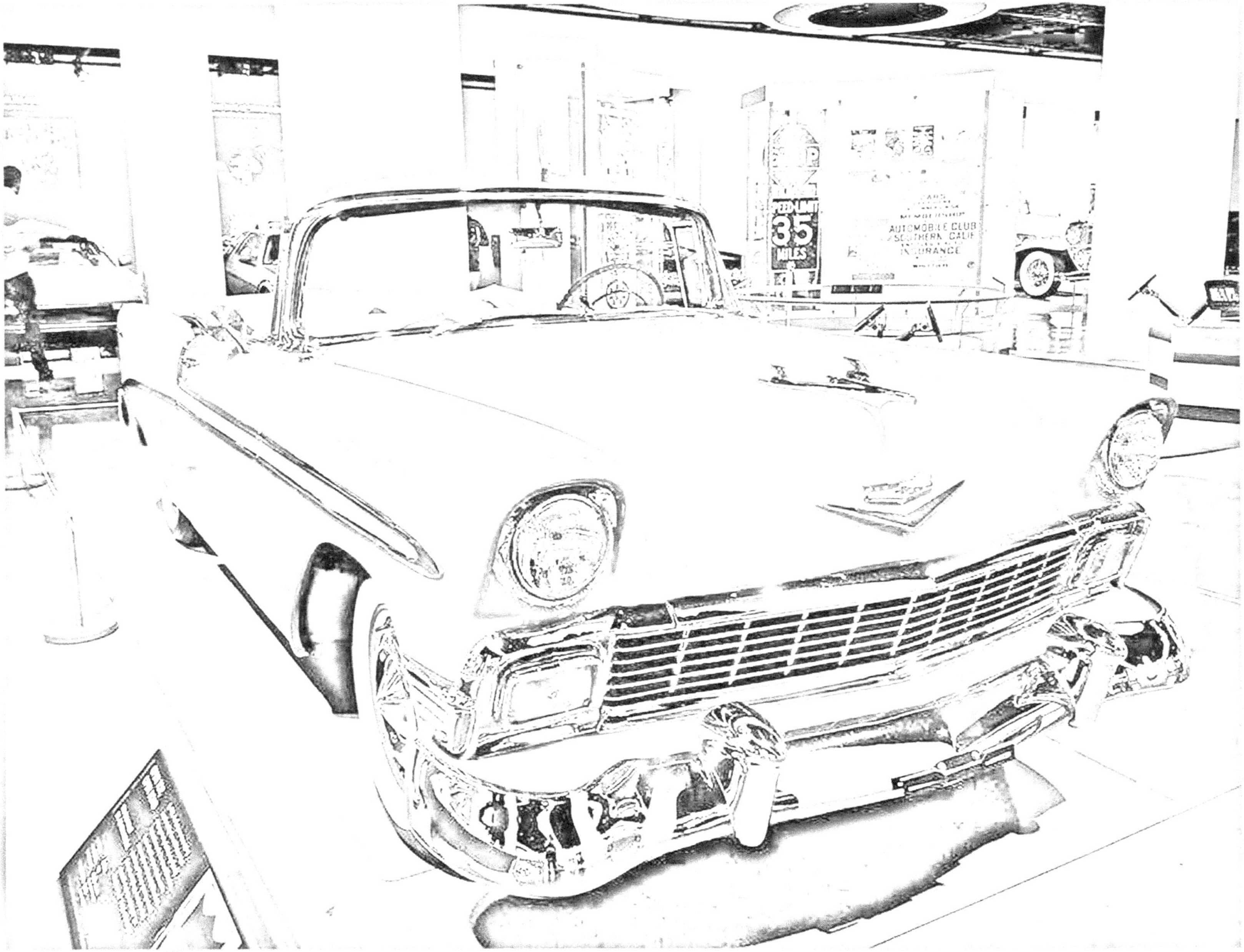
SPEED LIMIT
35
MILES
AUTOMOBILE CLUB
SOUTHERN CALIF
INSURANCE

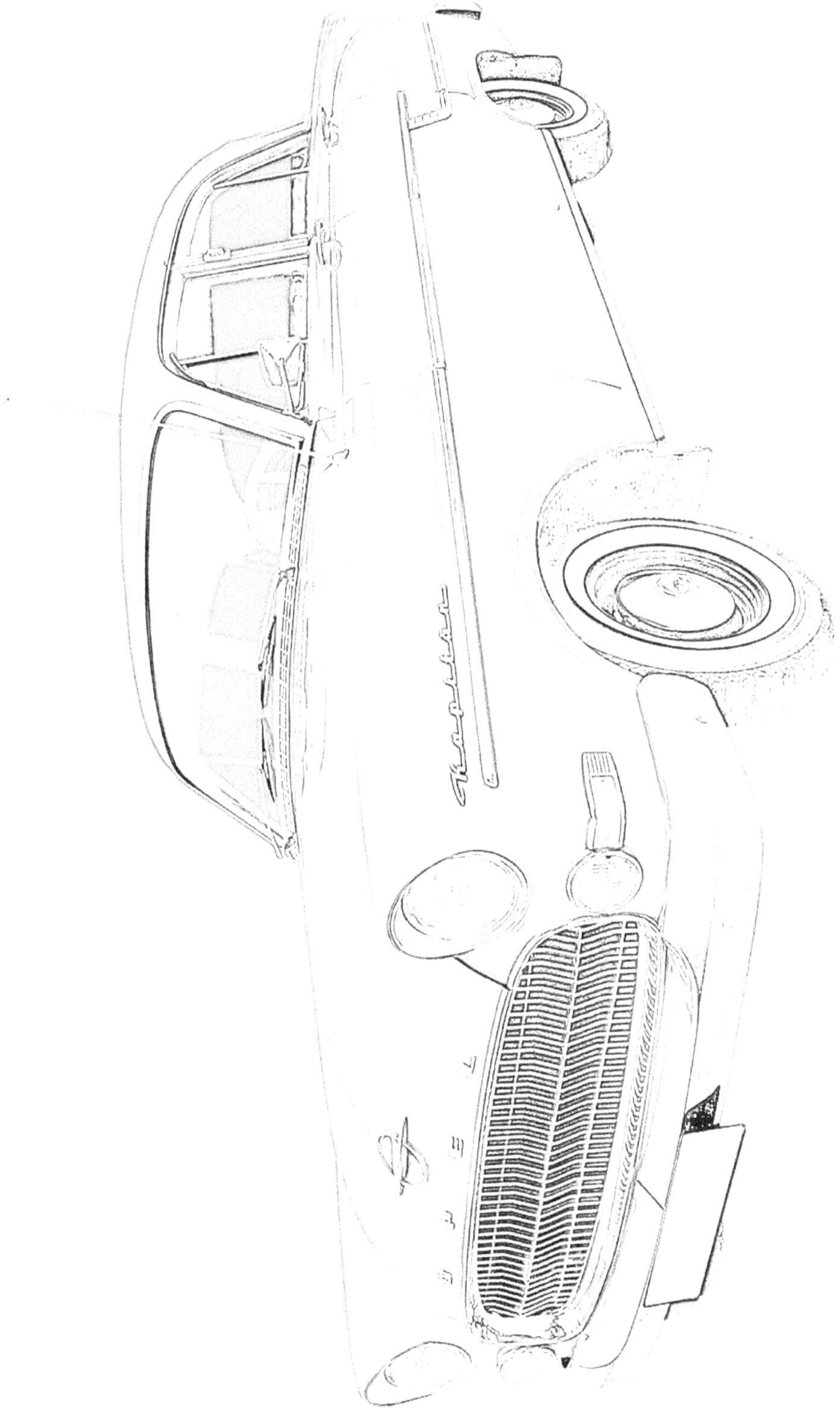

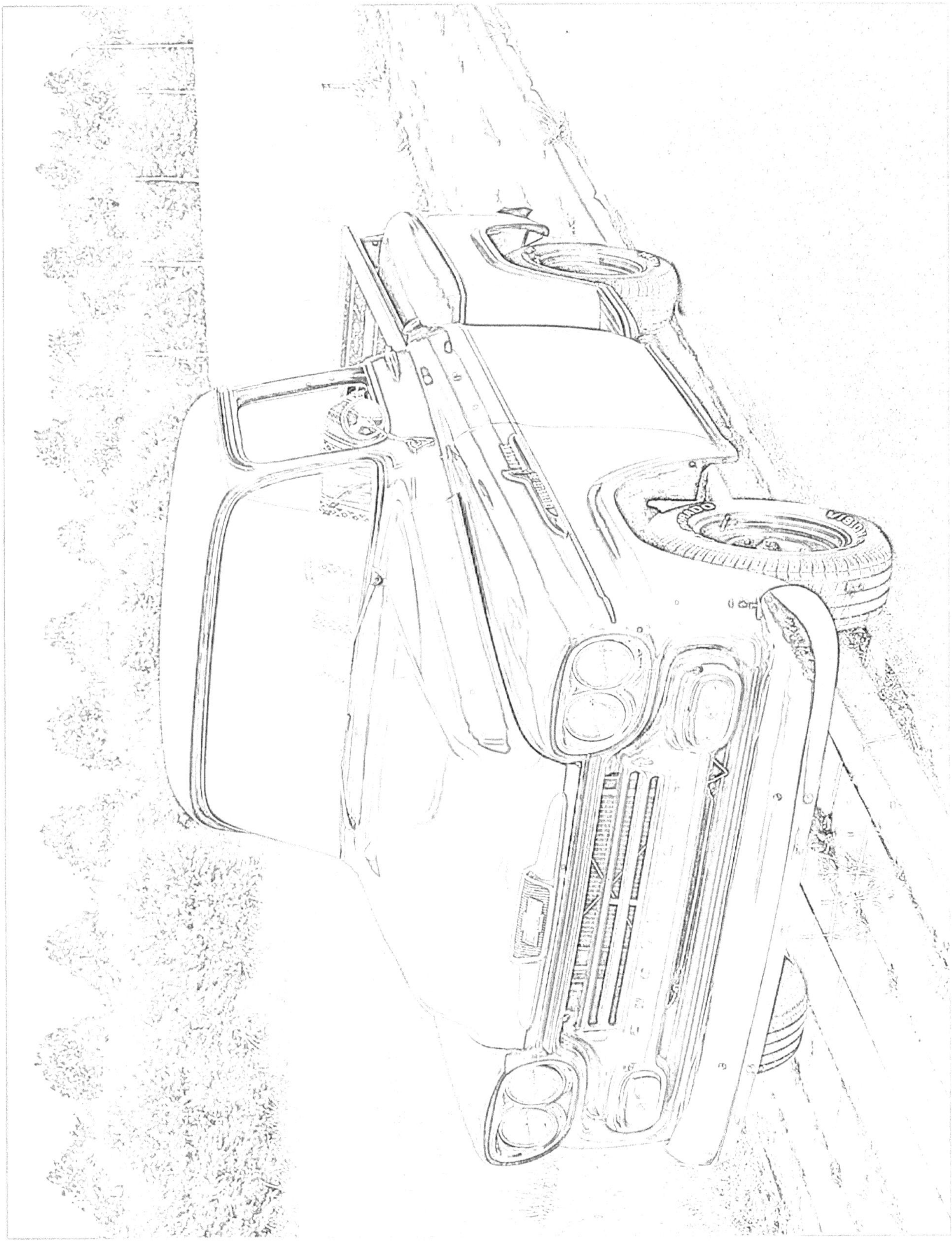

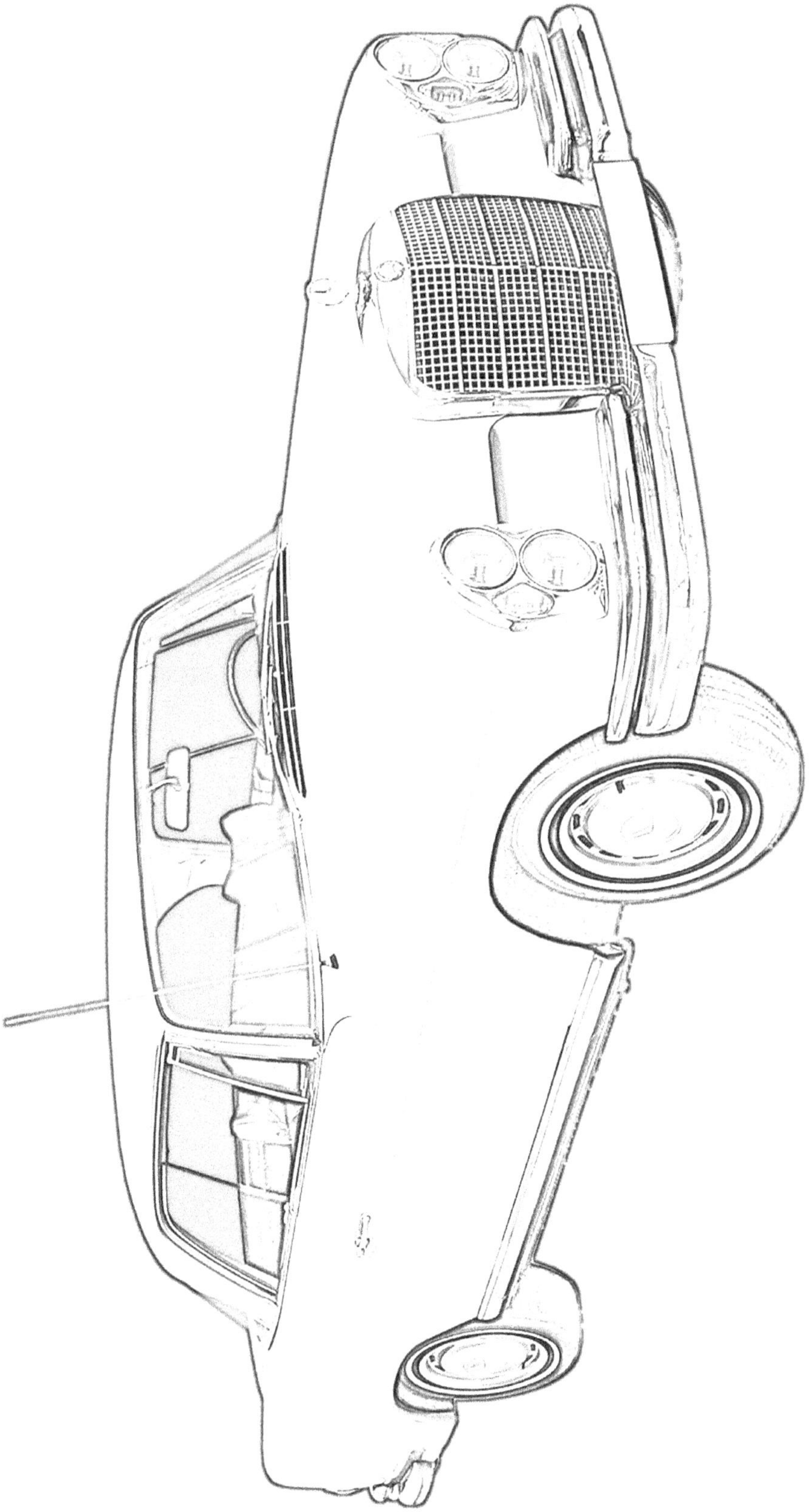

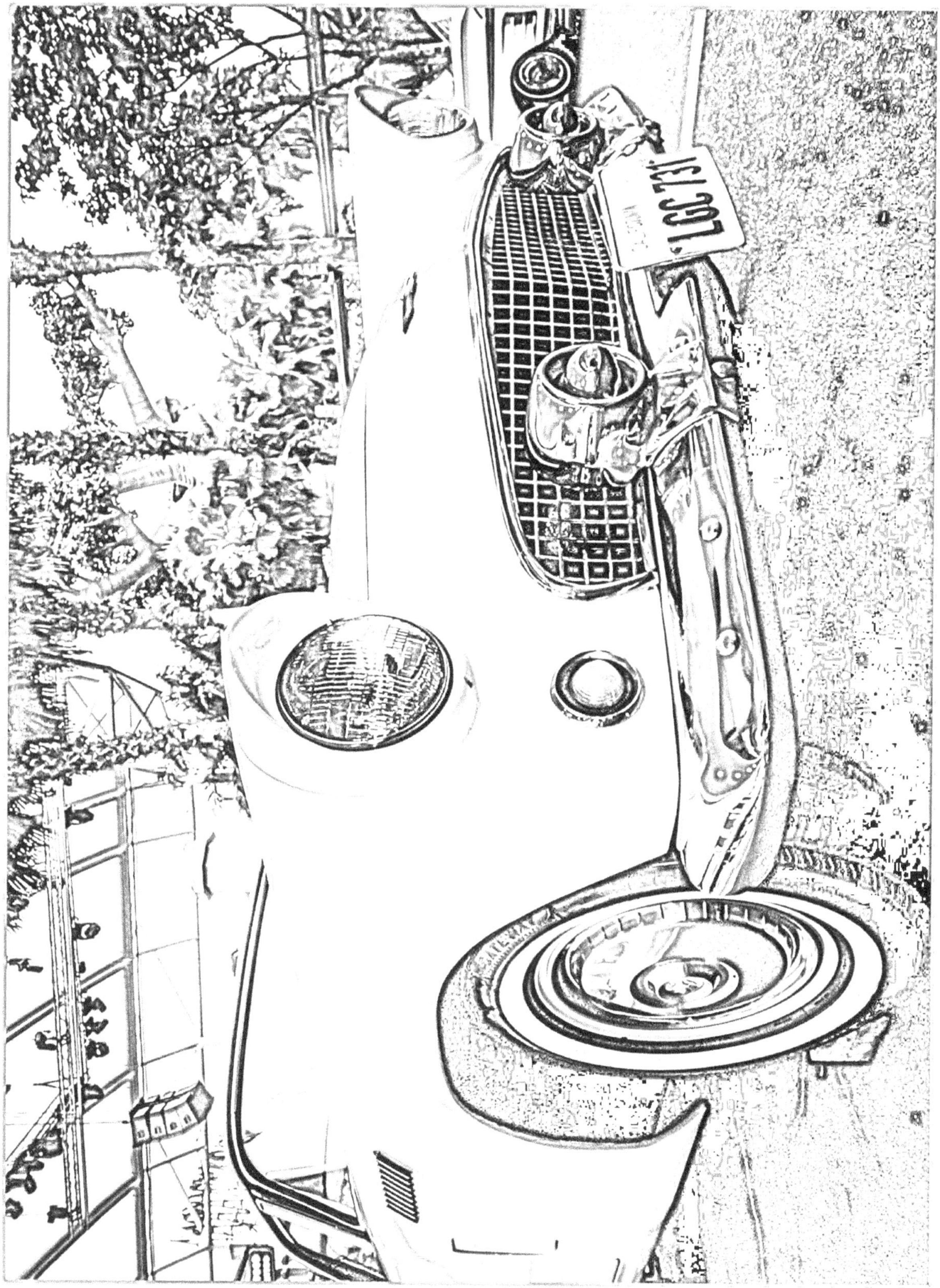

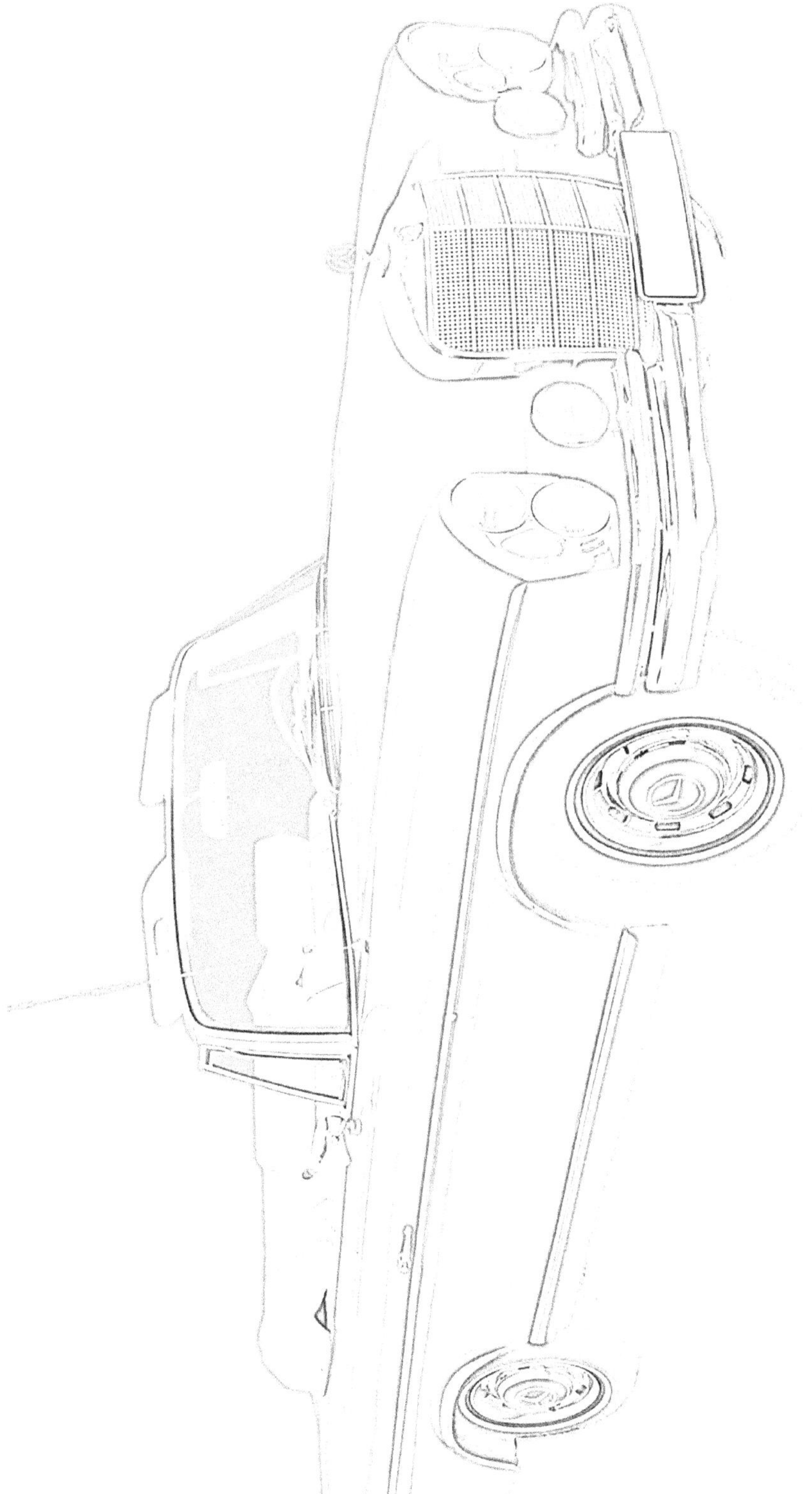

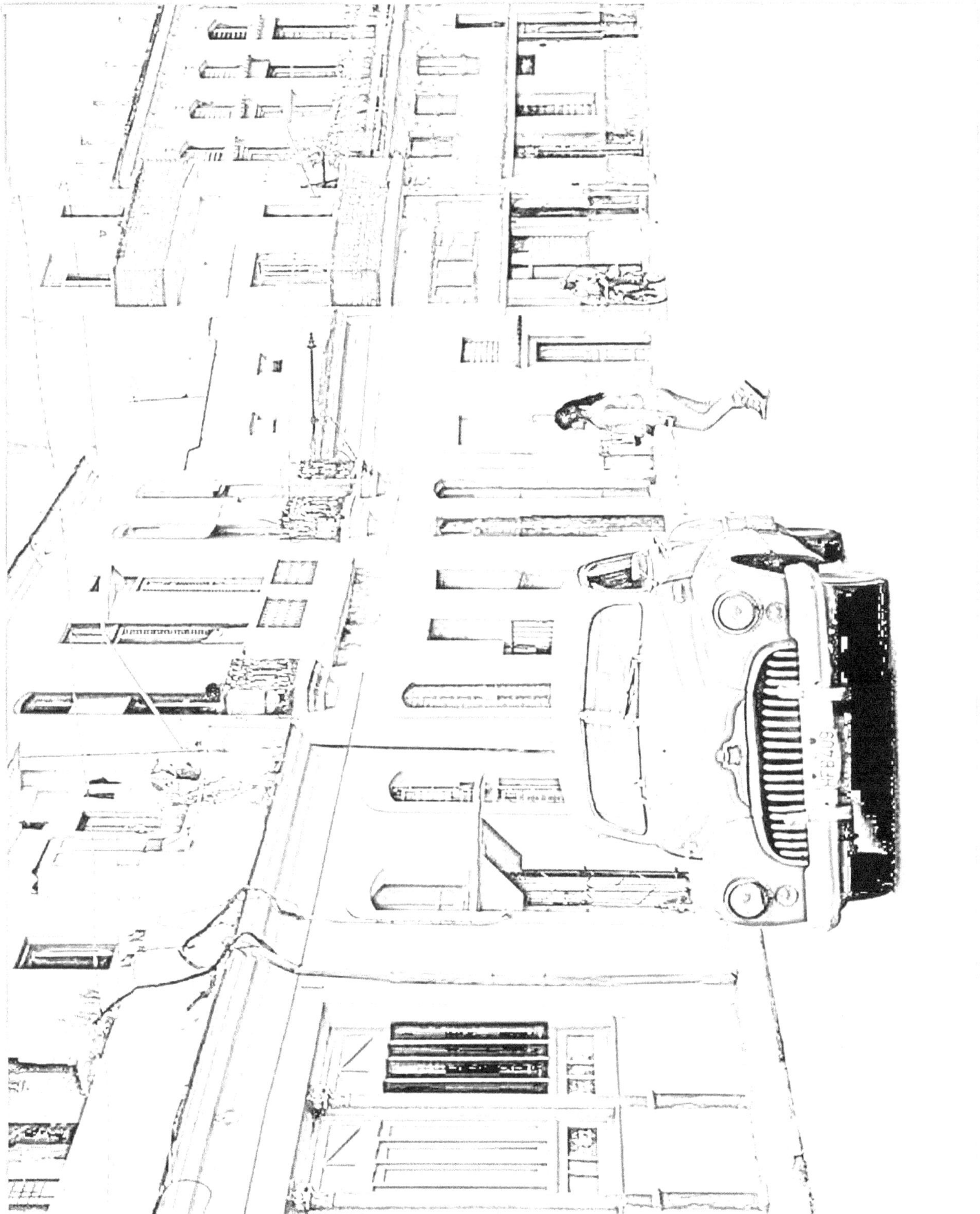

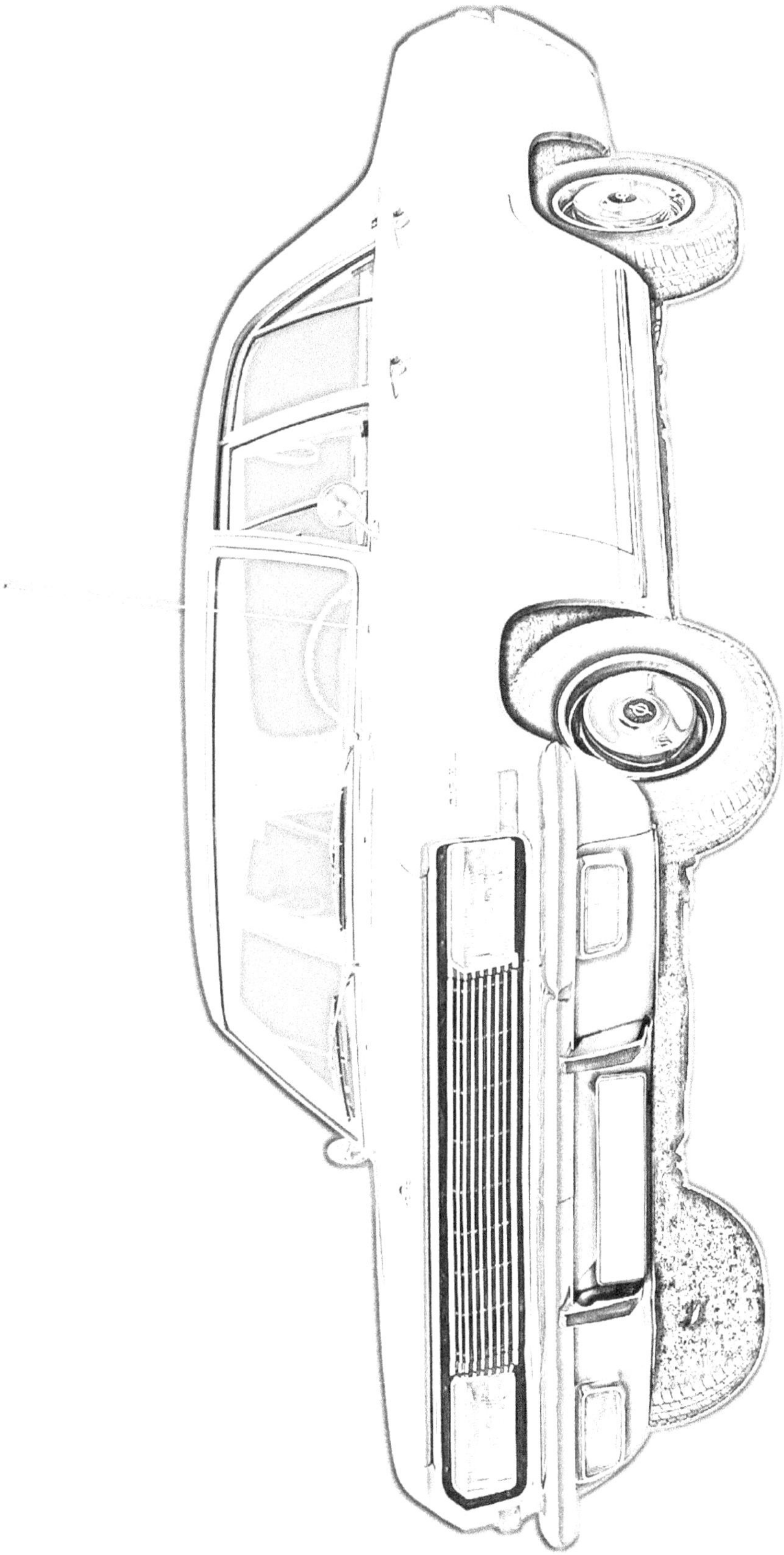

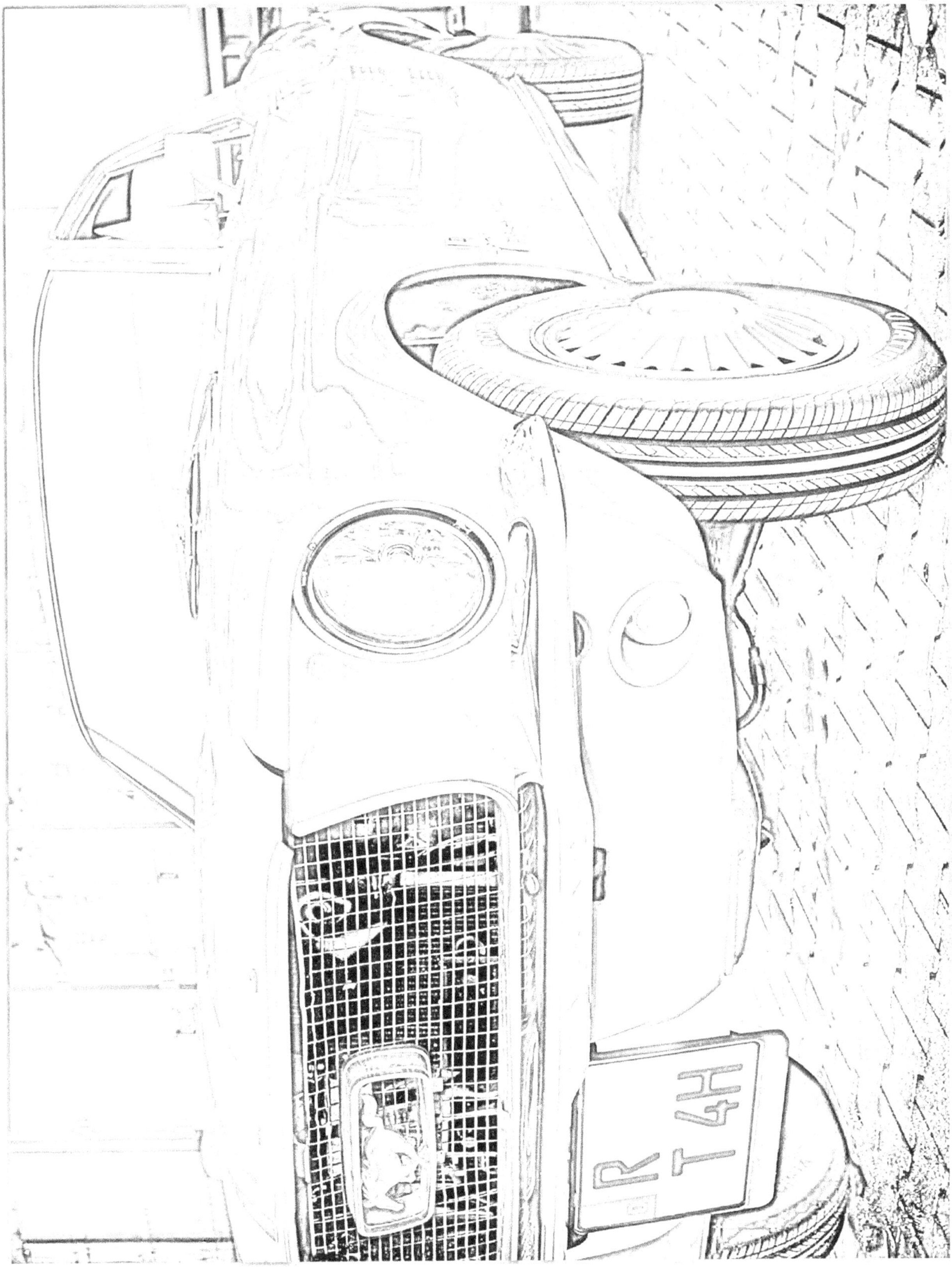
R
T4H

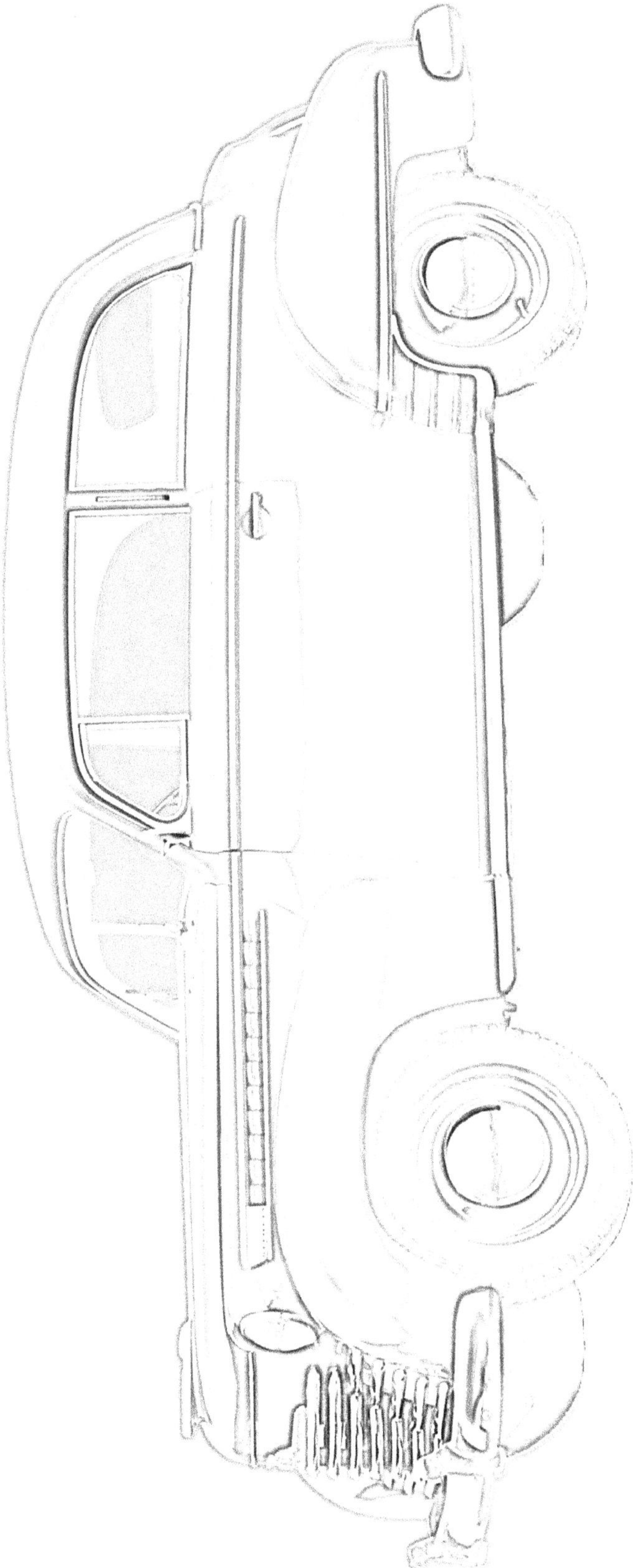

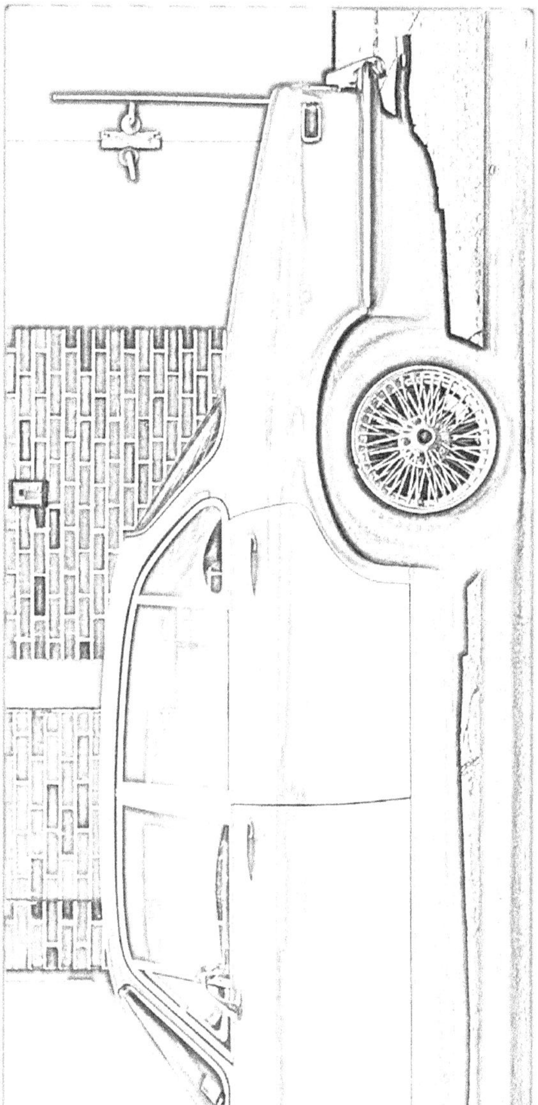

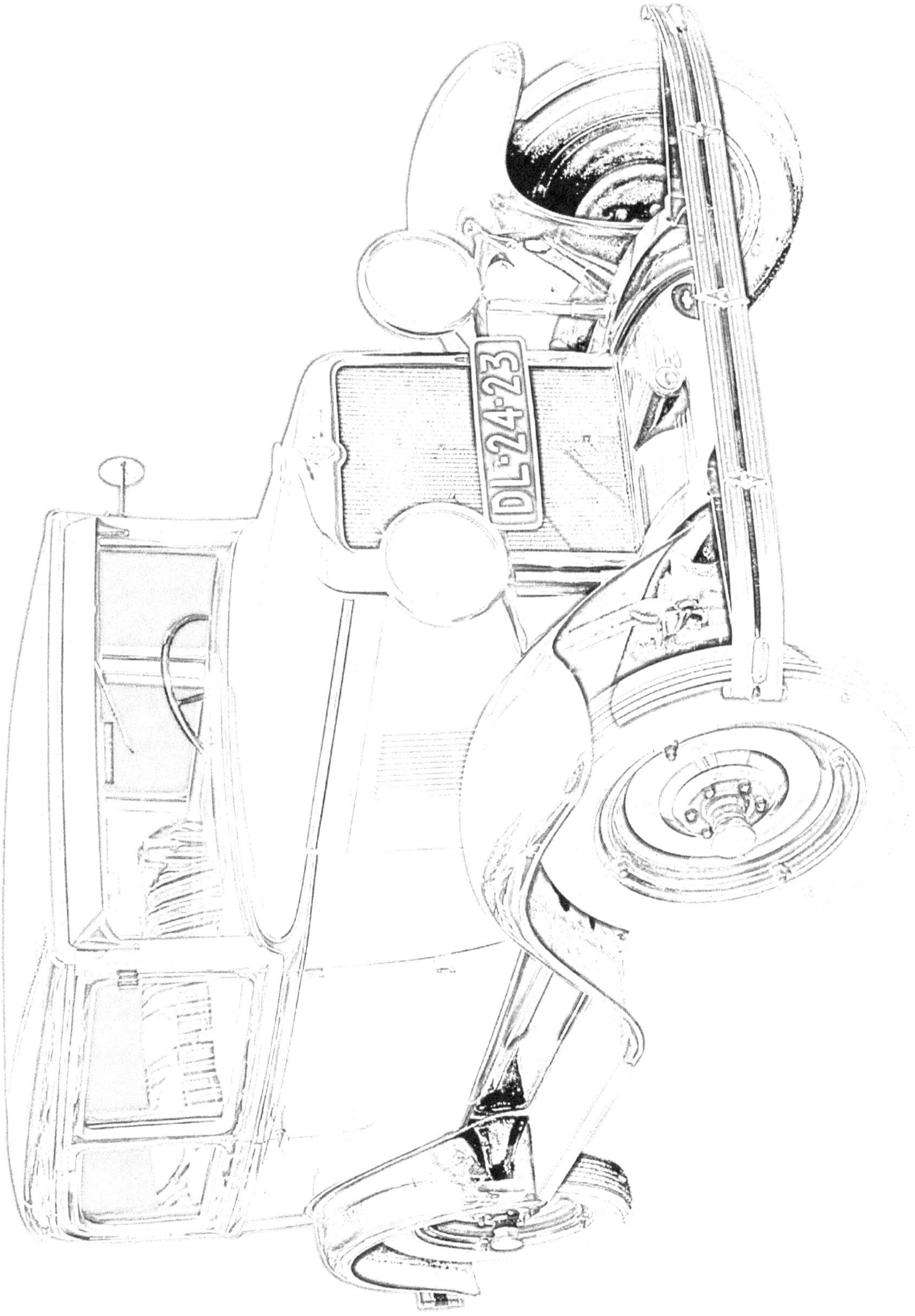
DL·24·23

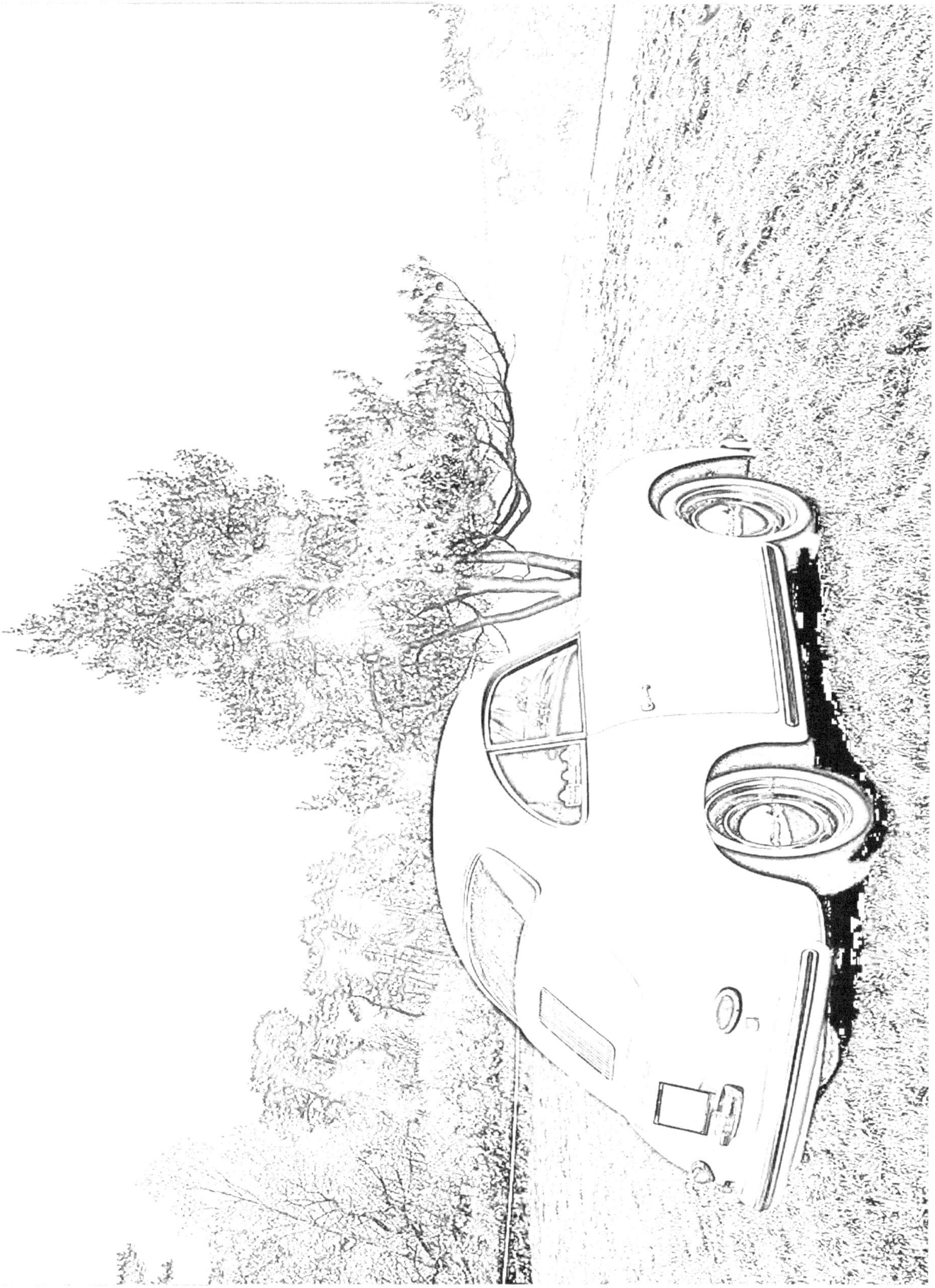

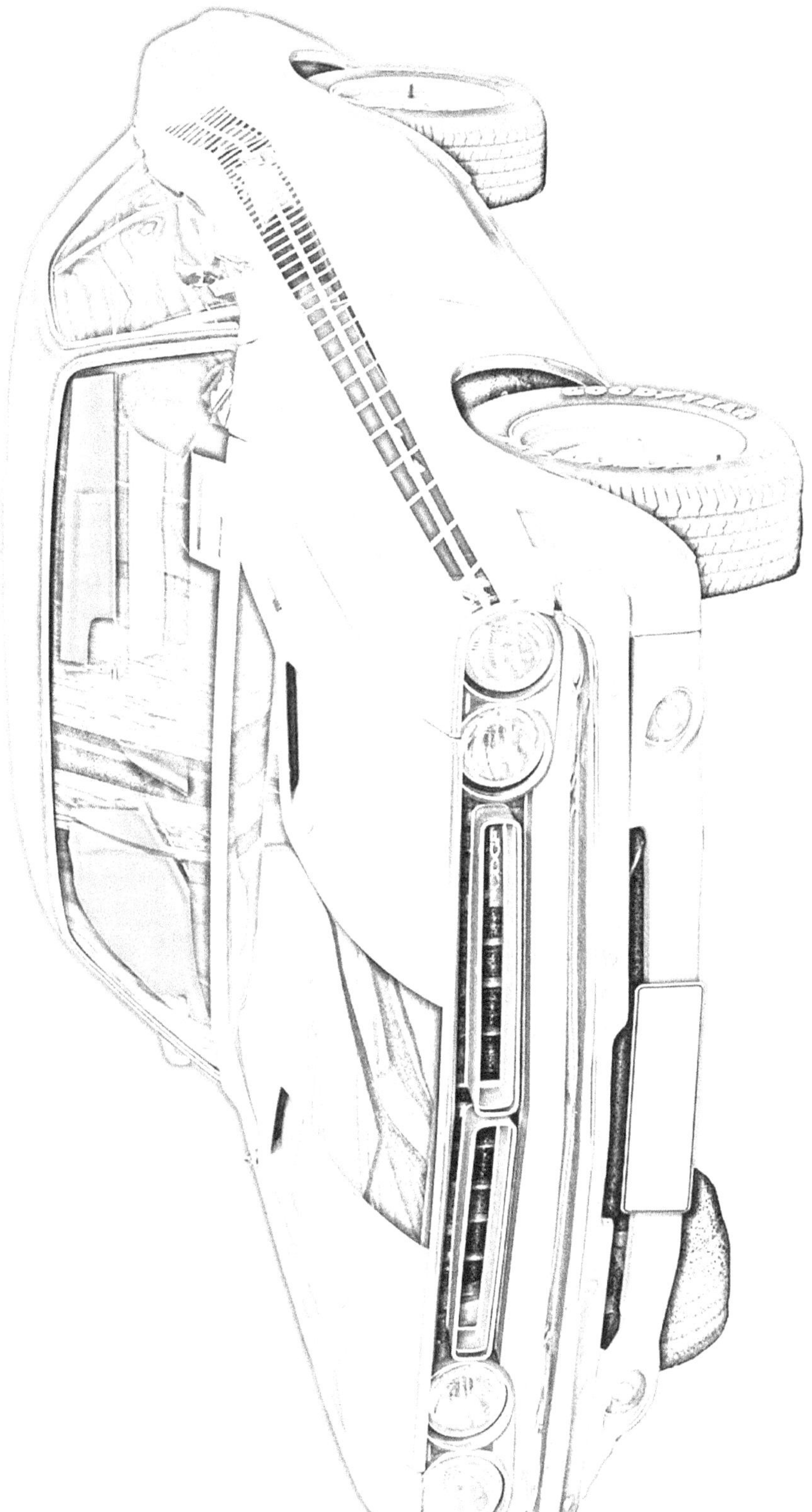

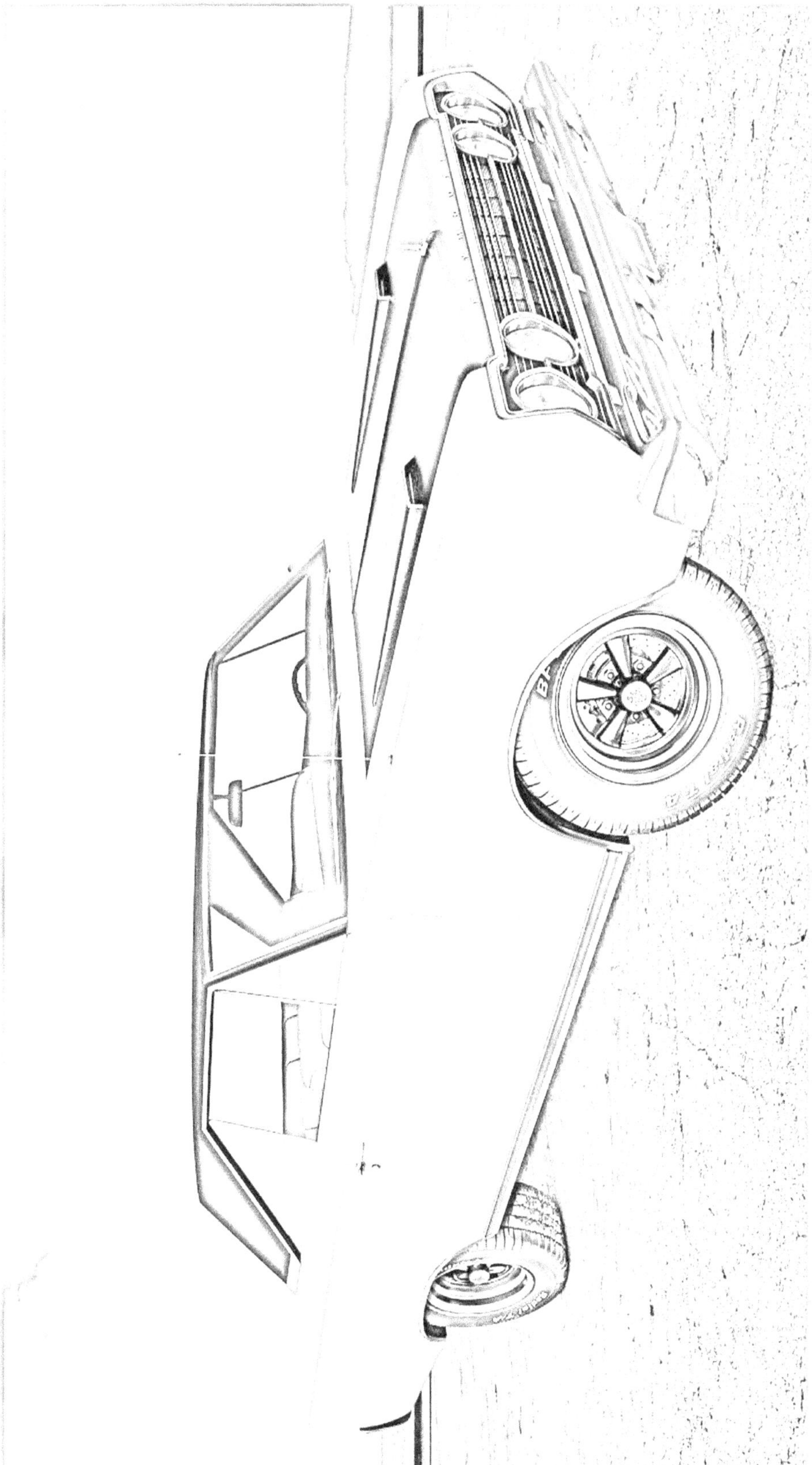

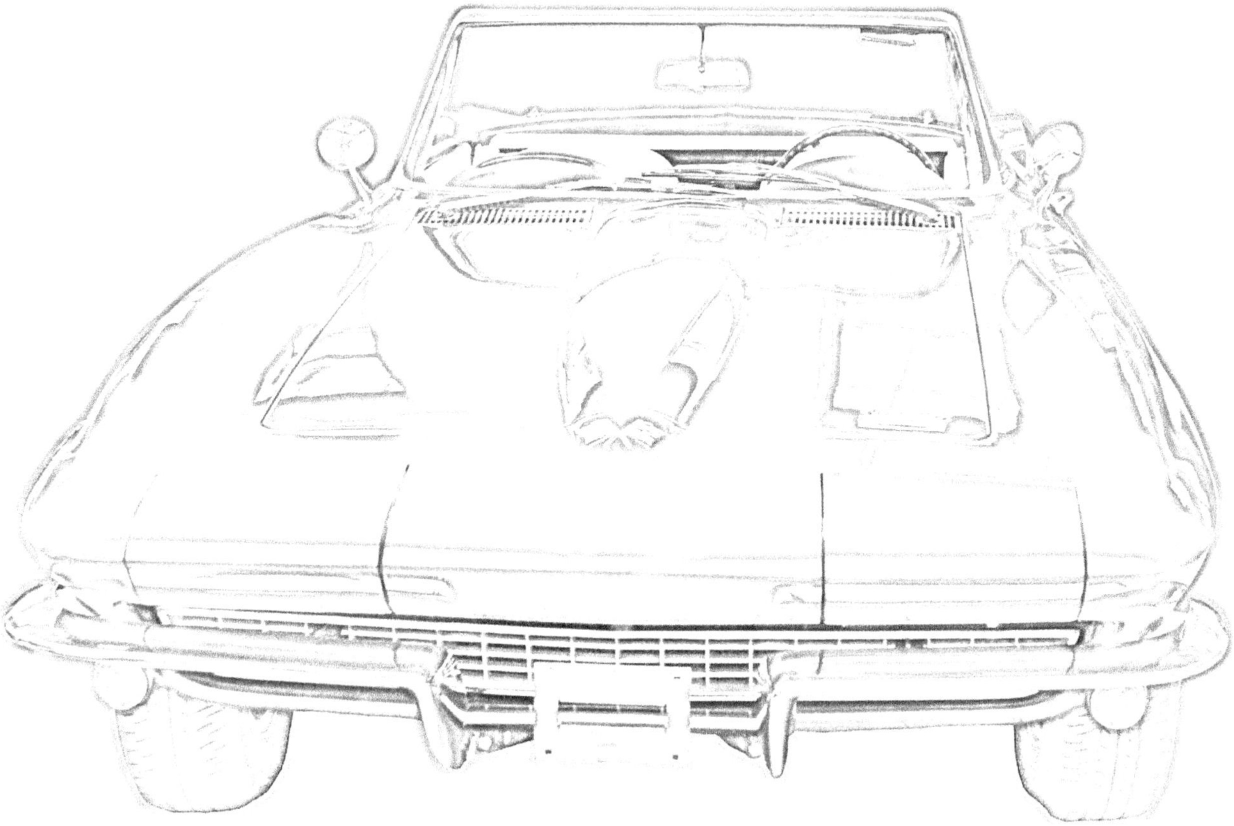

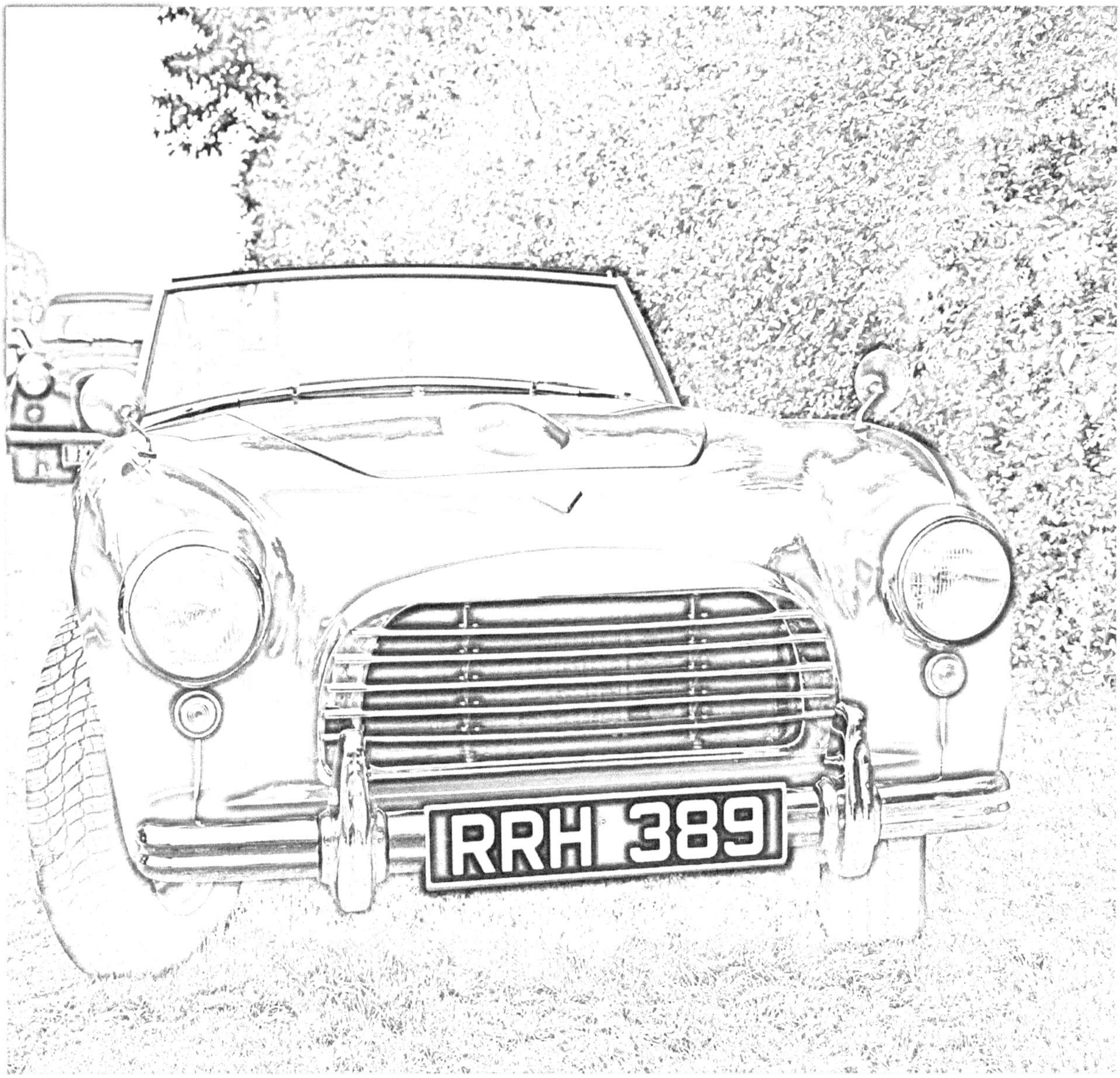
RRH 389

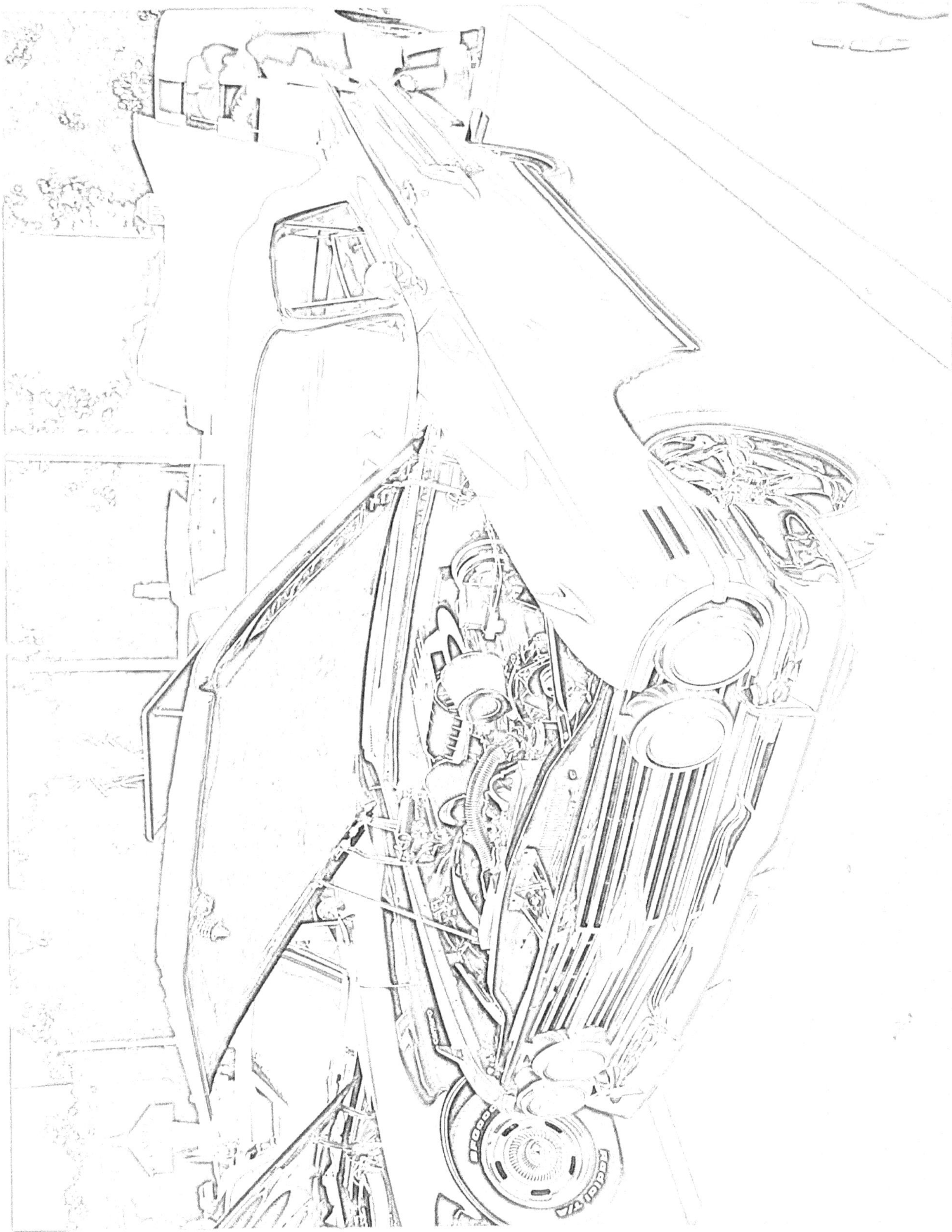

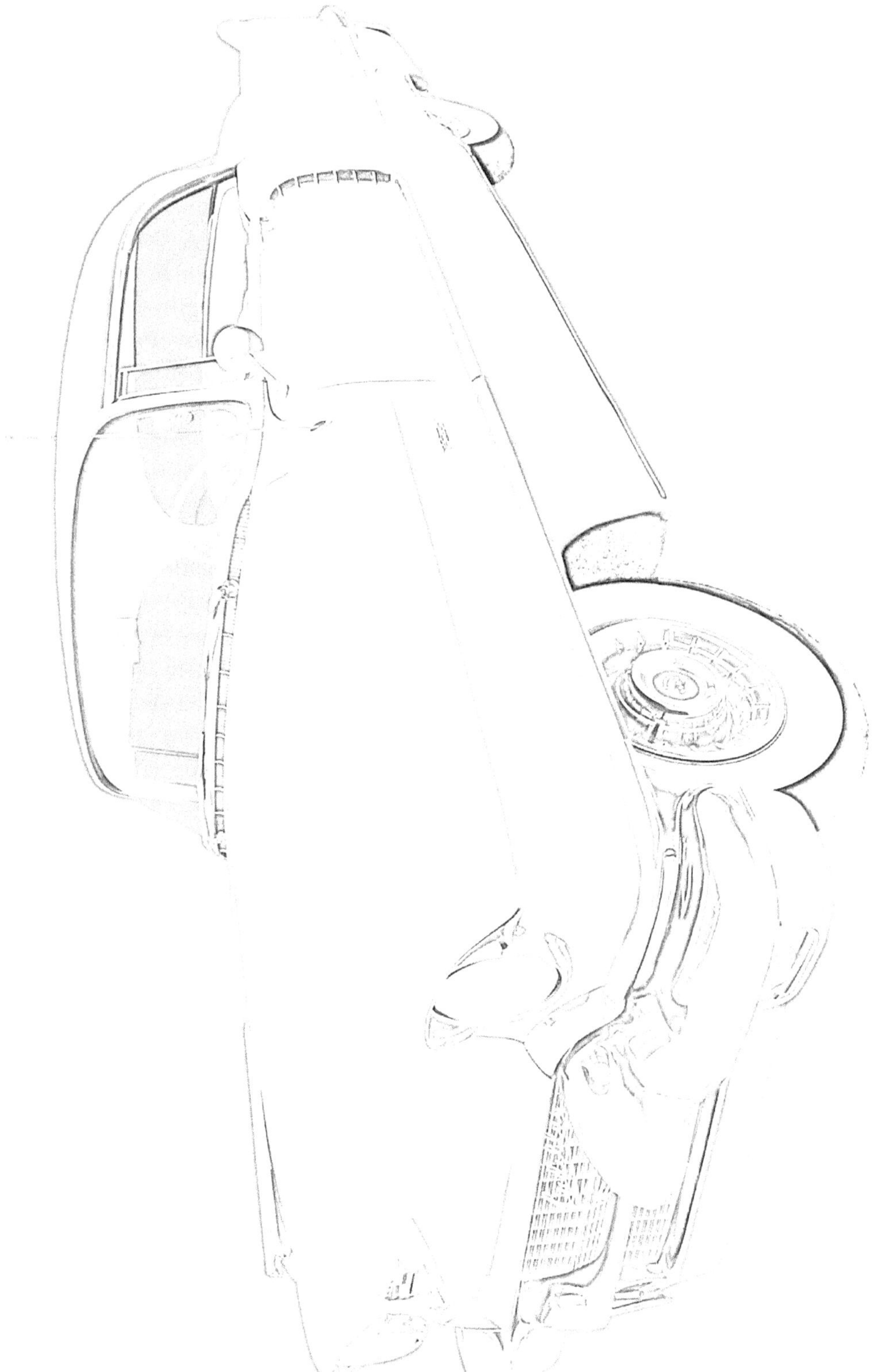

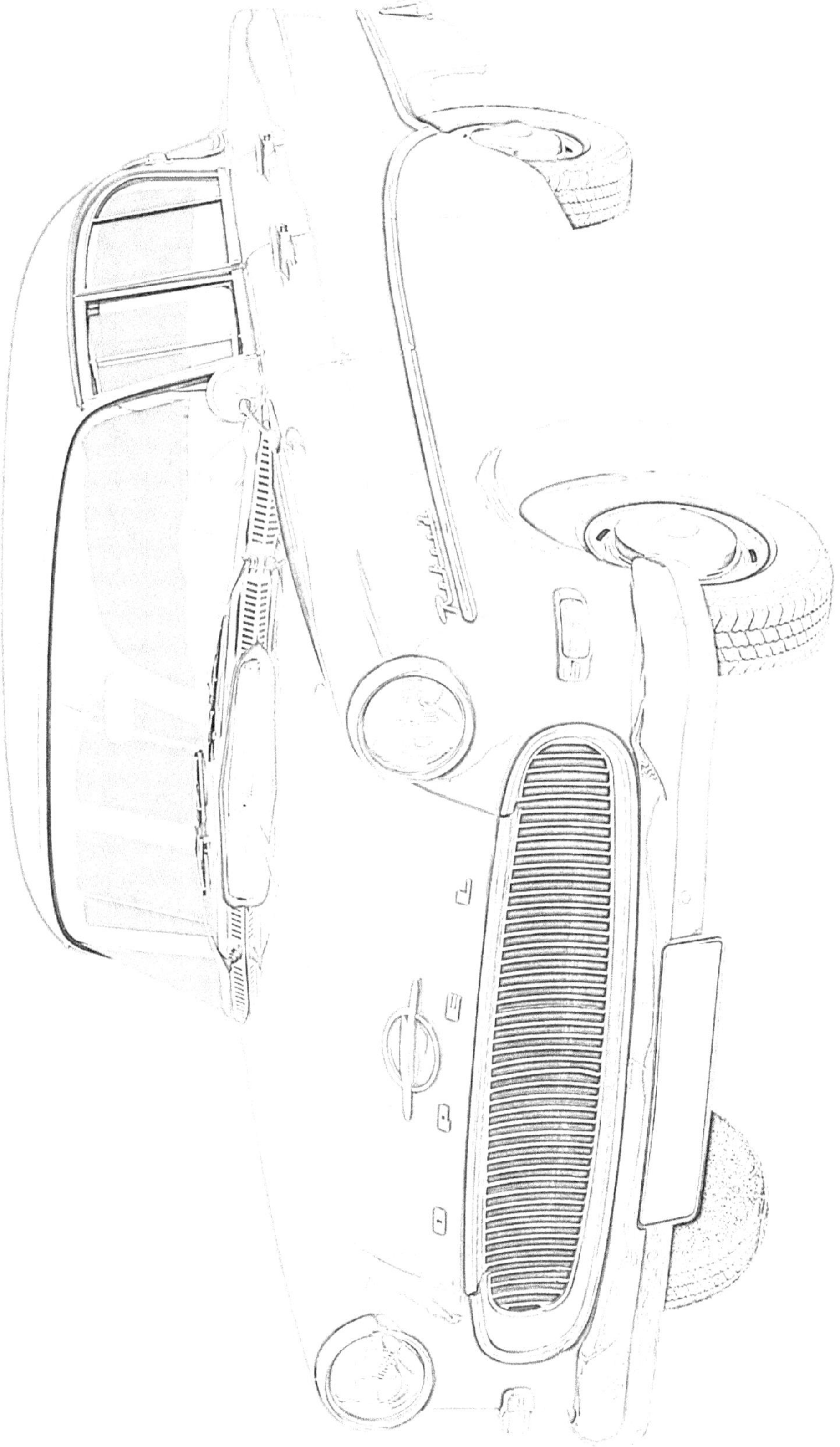

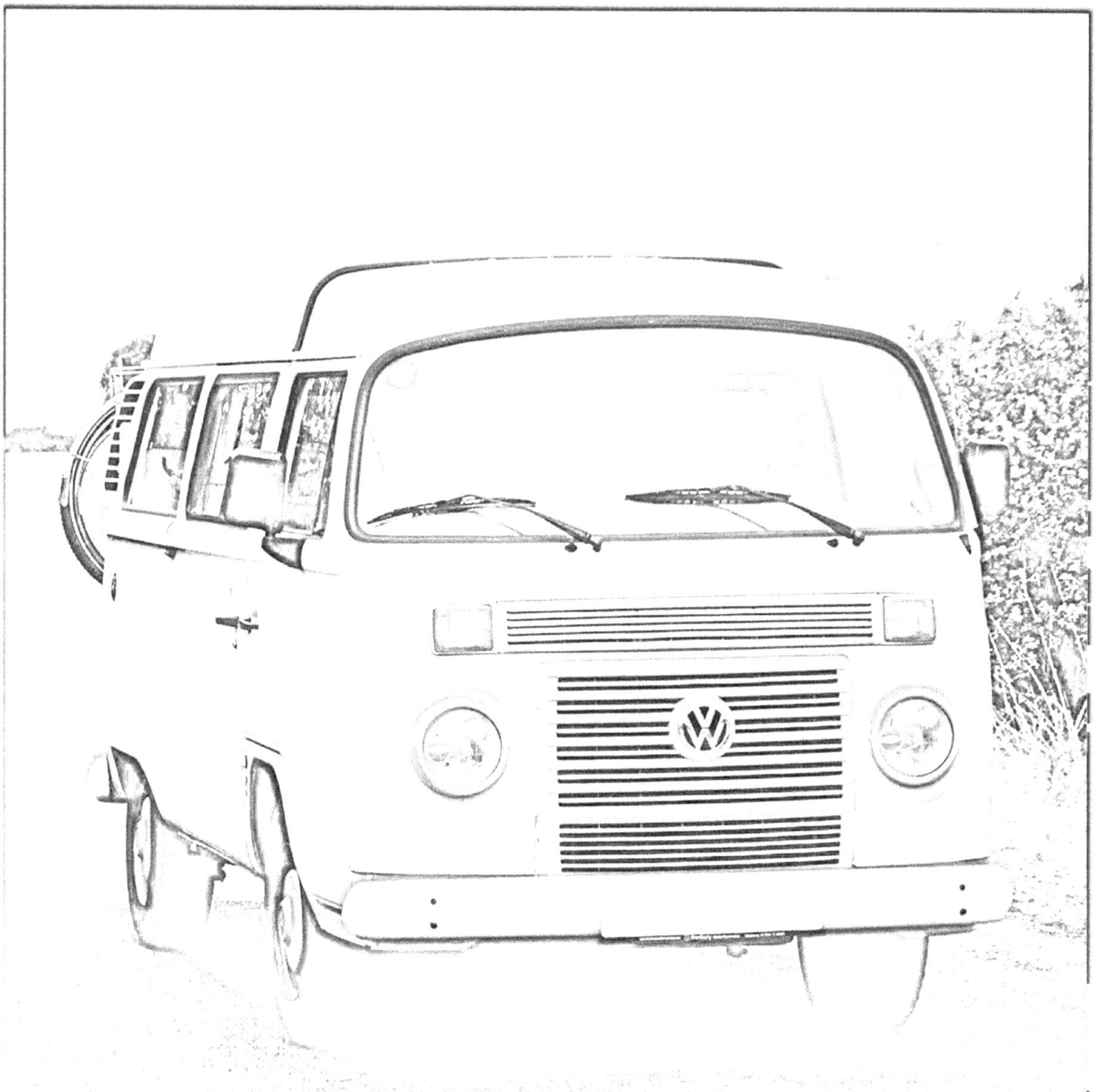

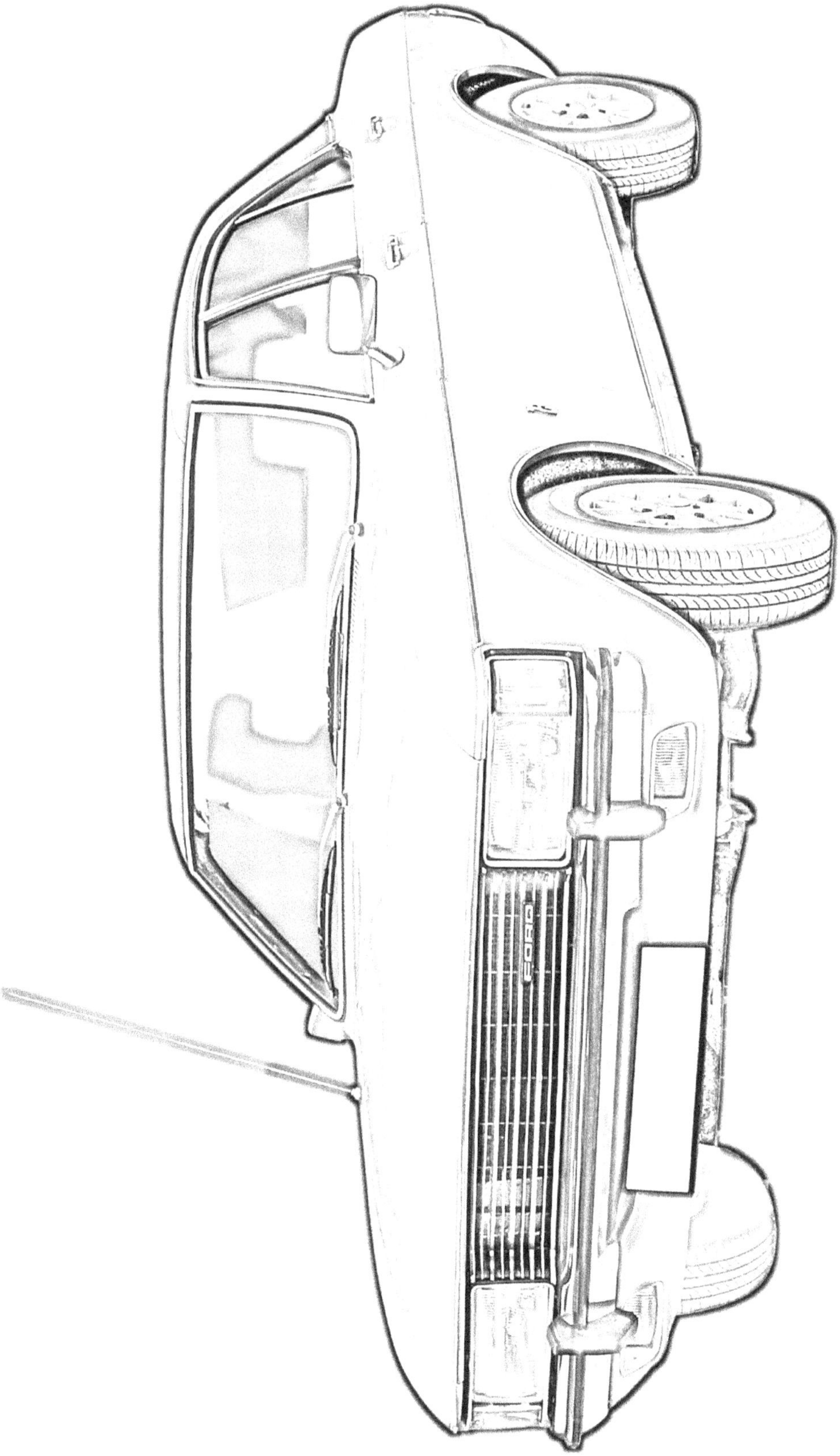

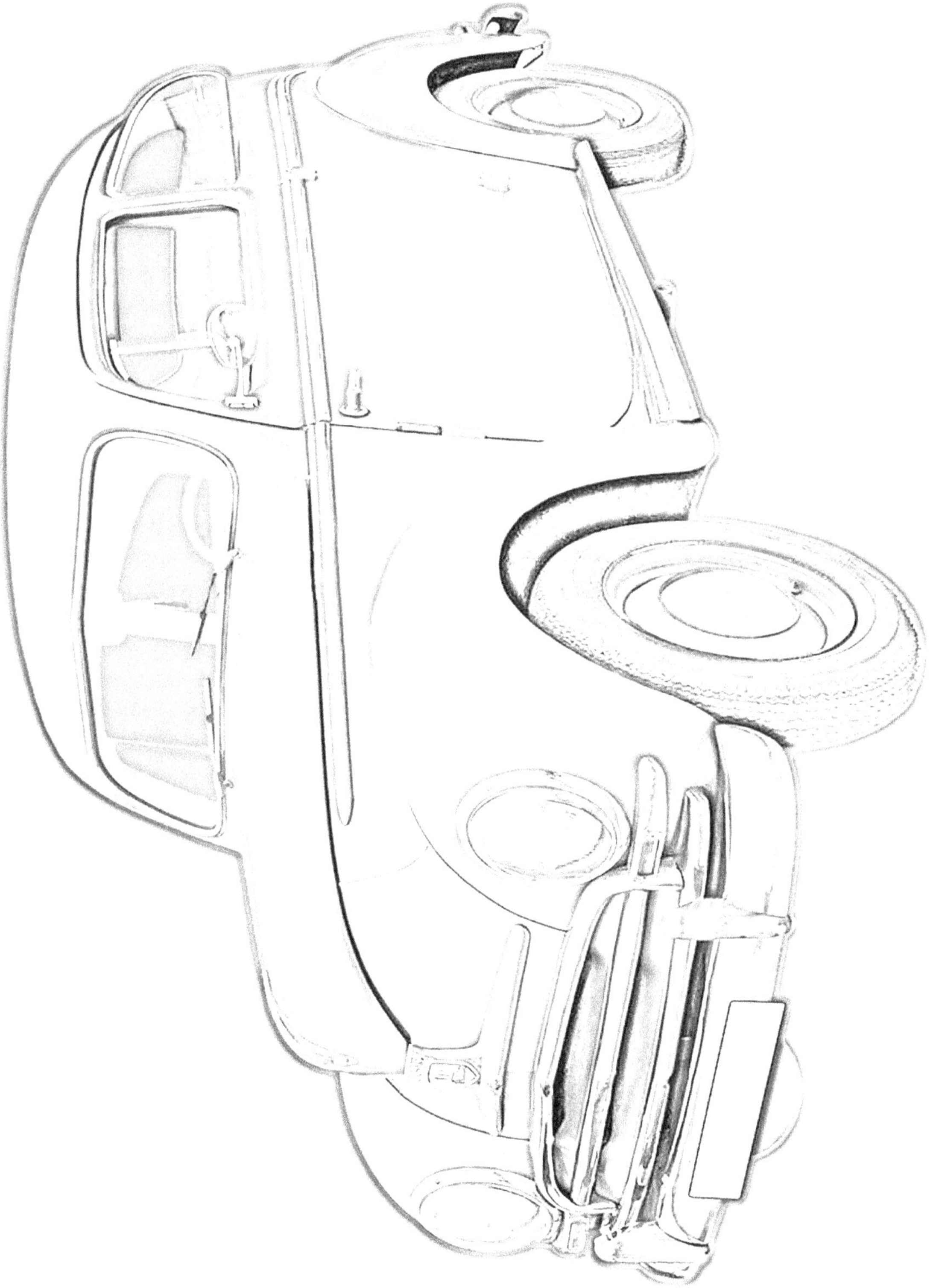

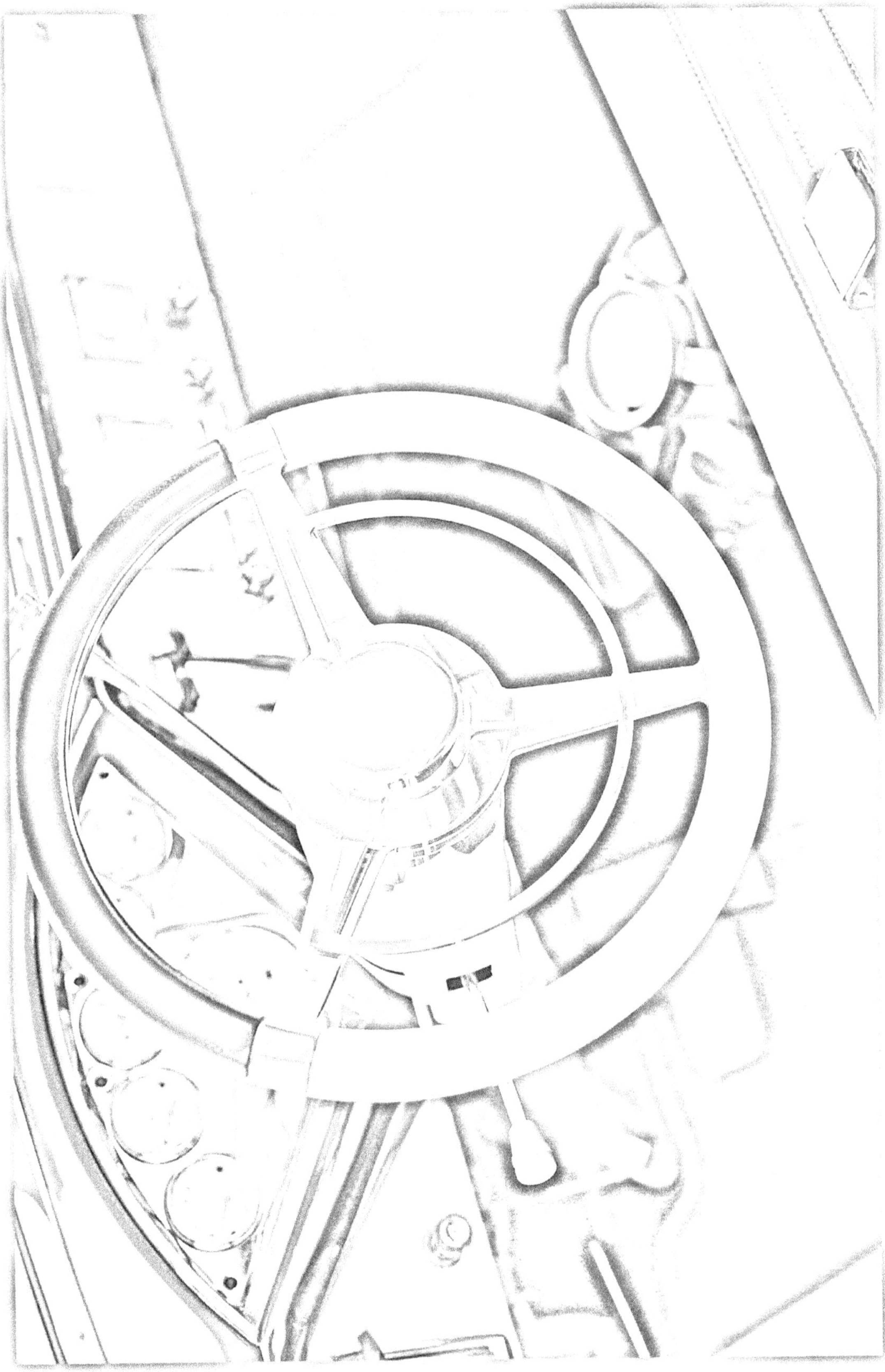

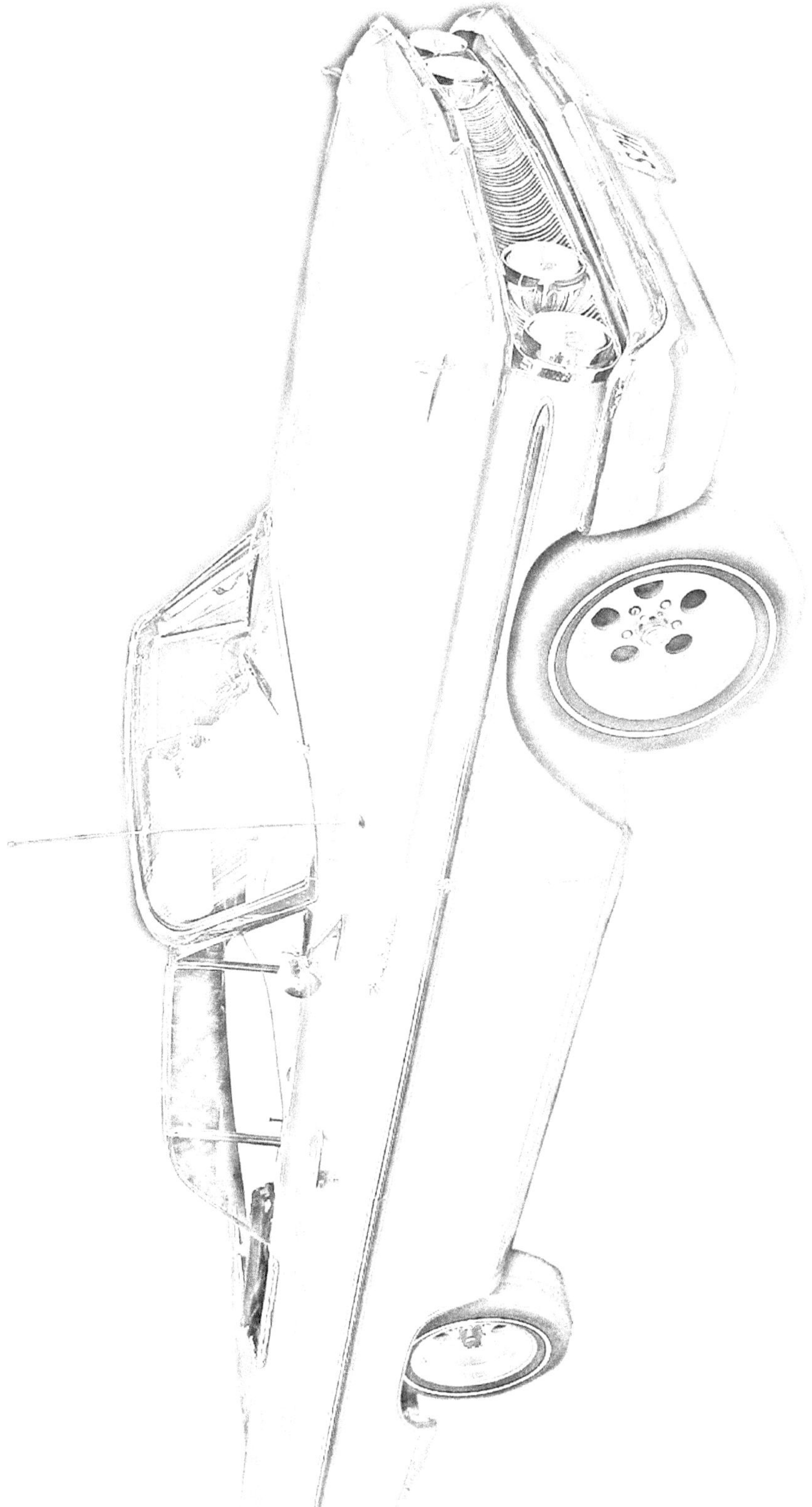

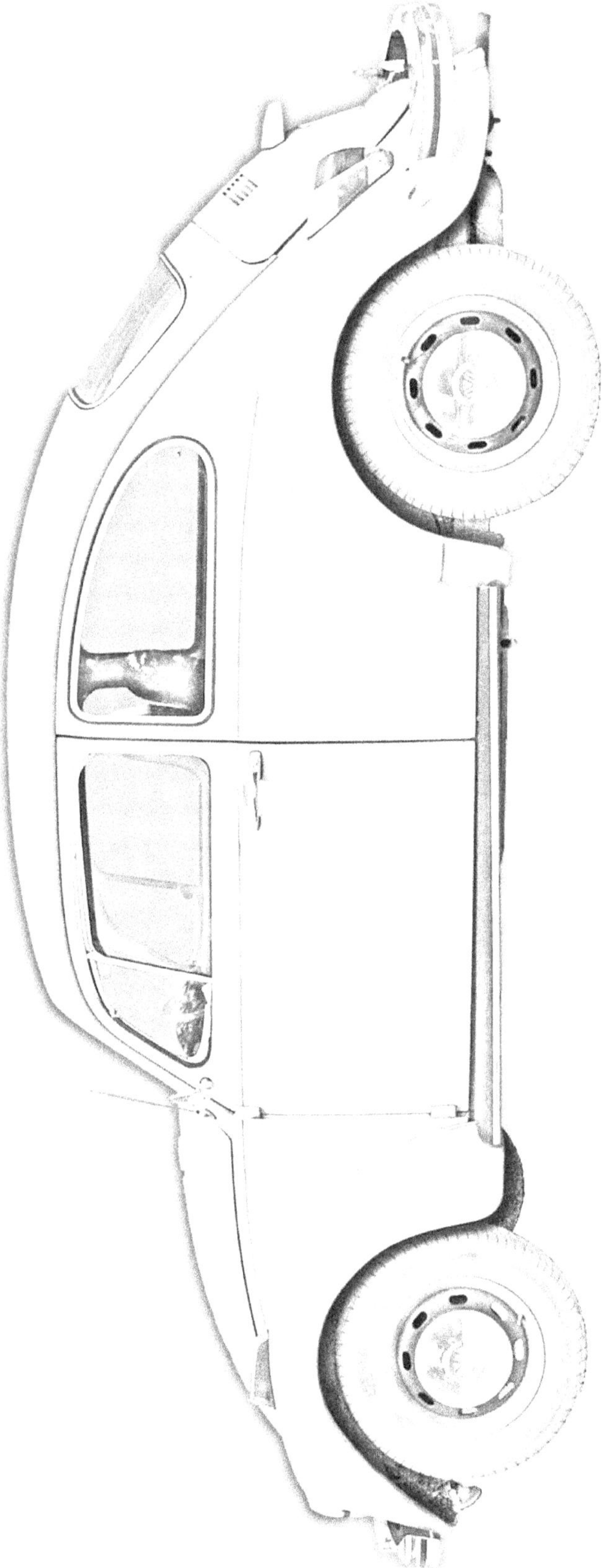

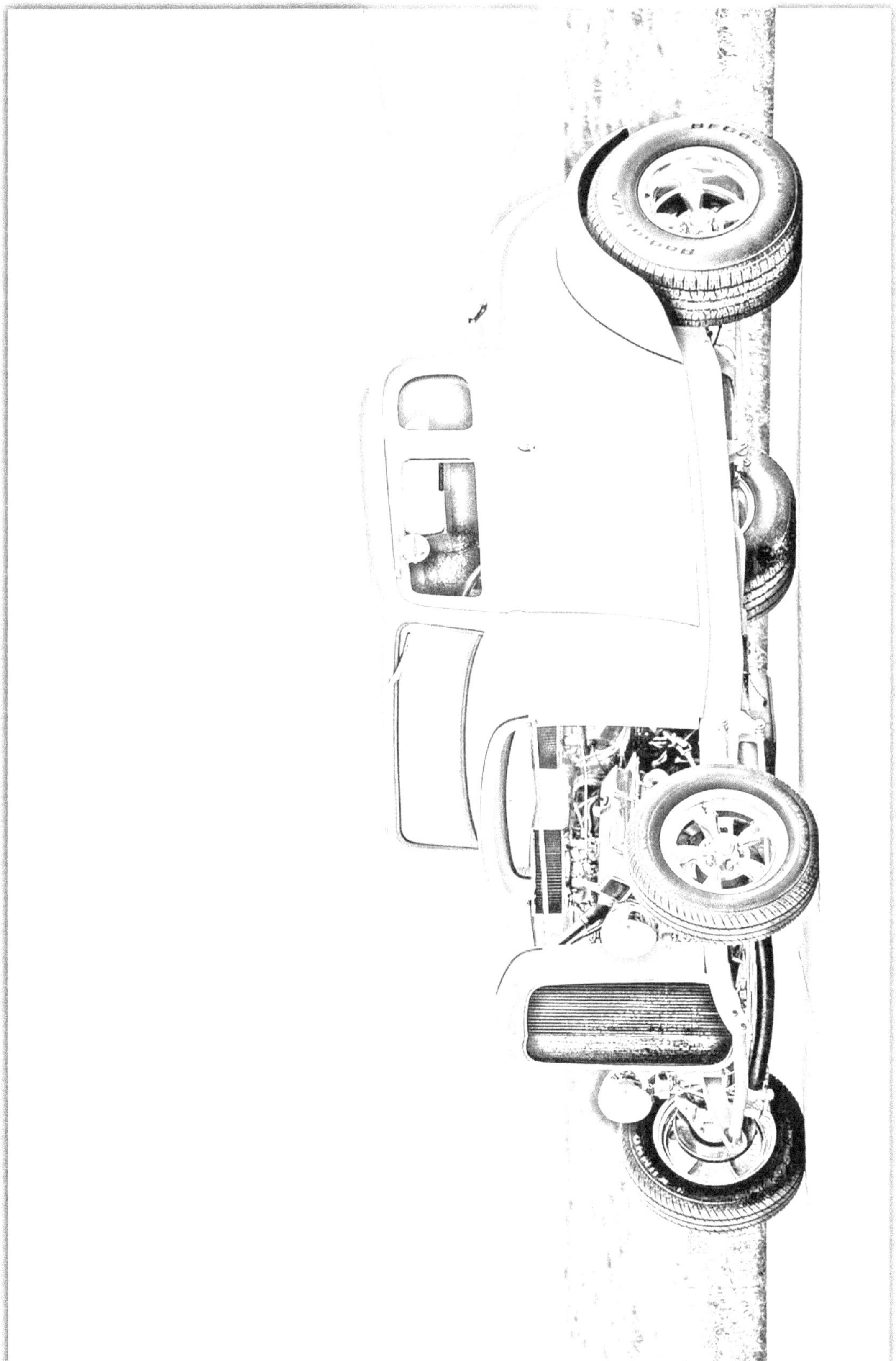

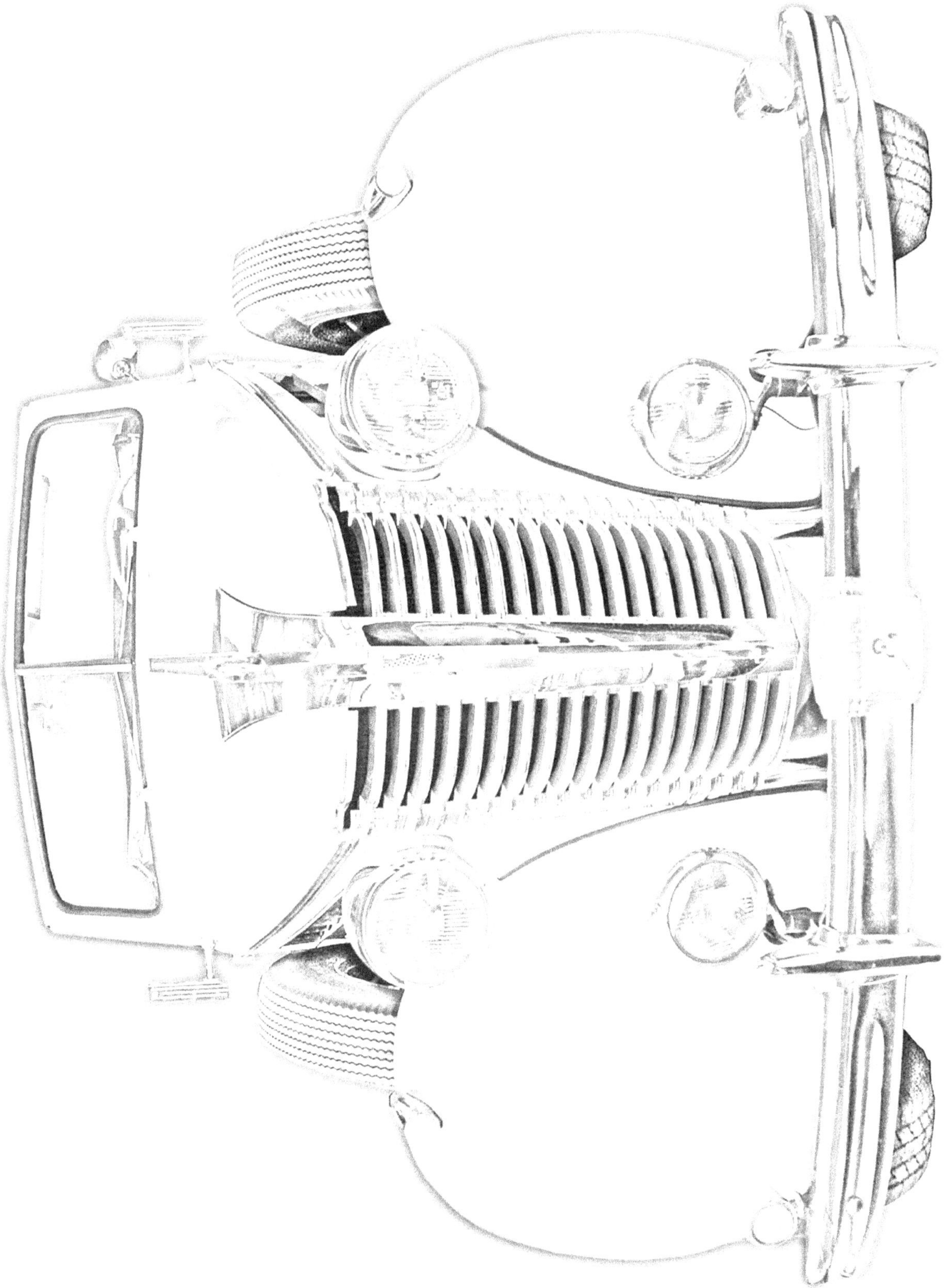

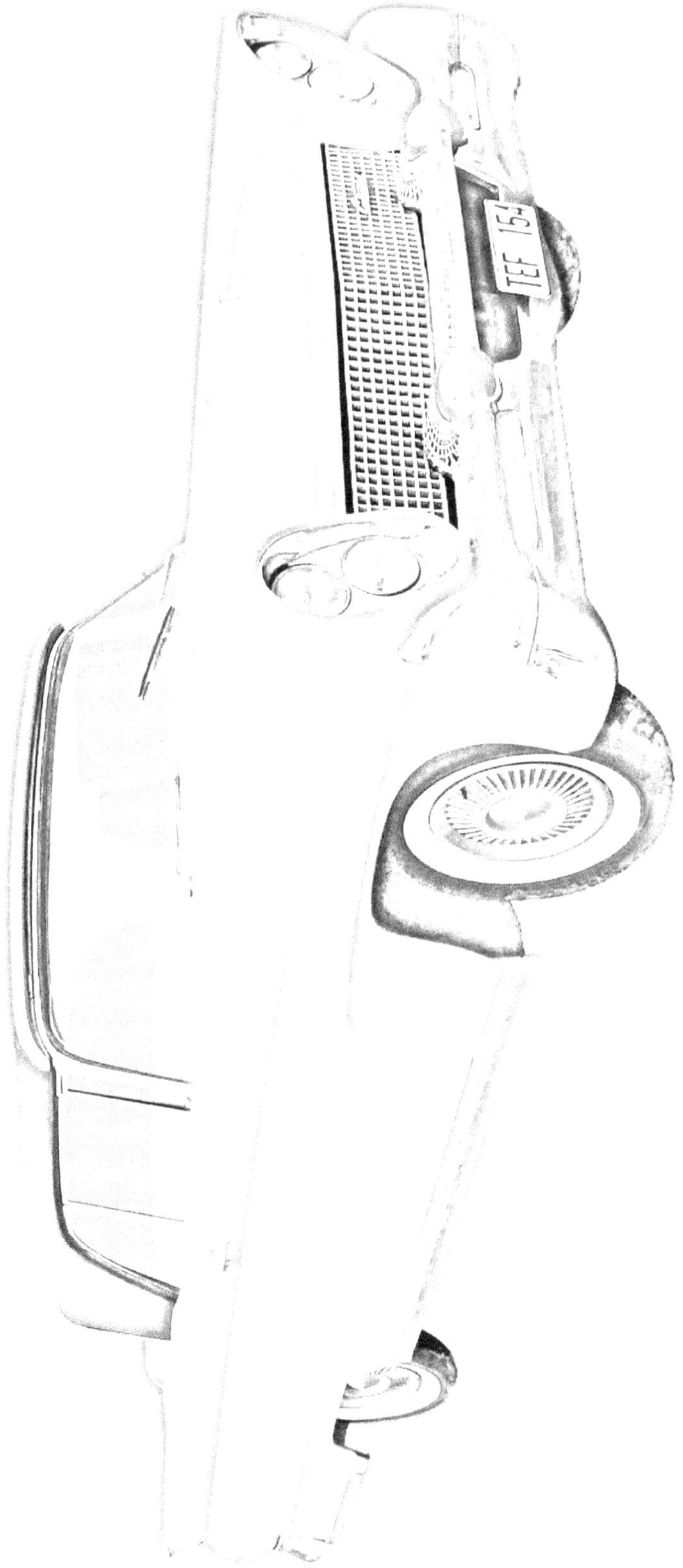

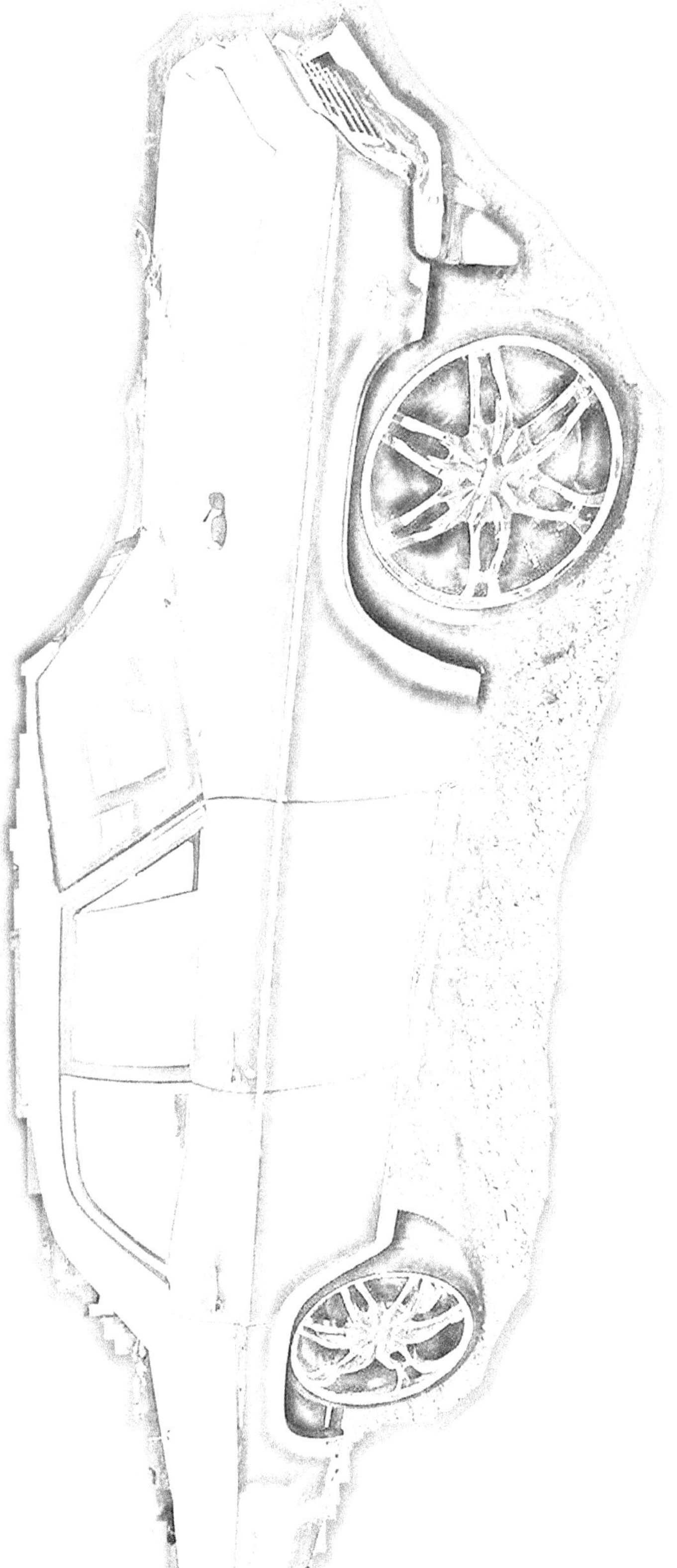

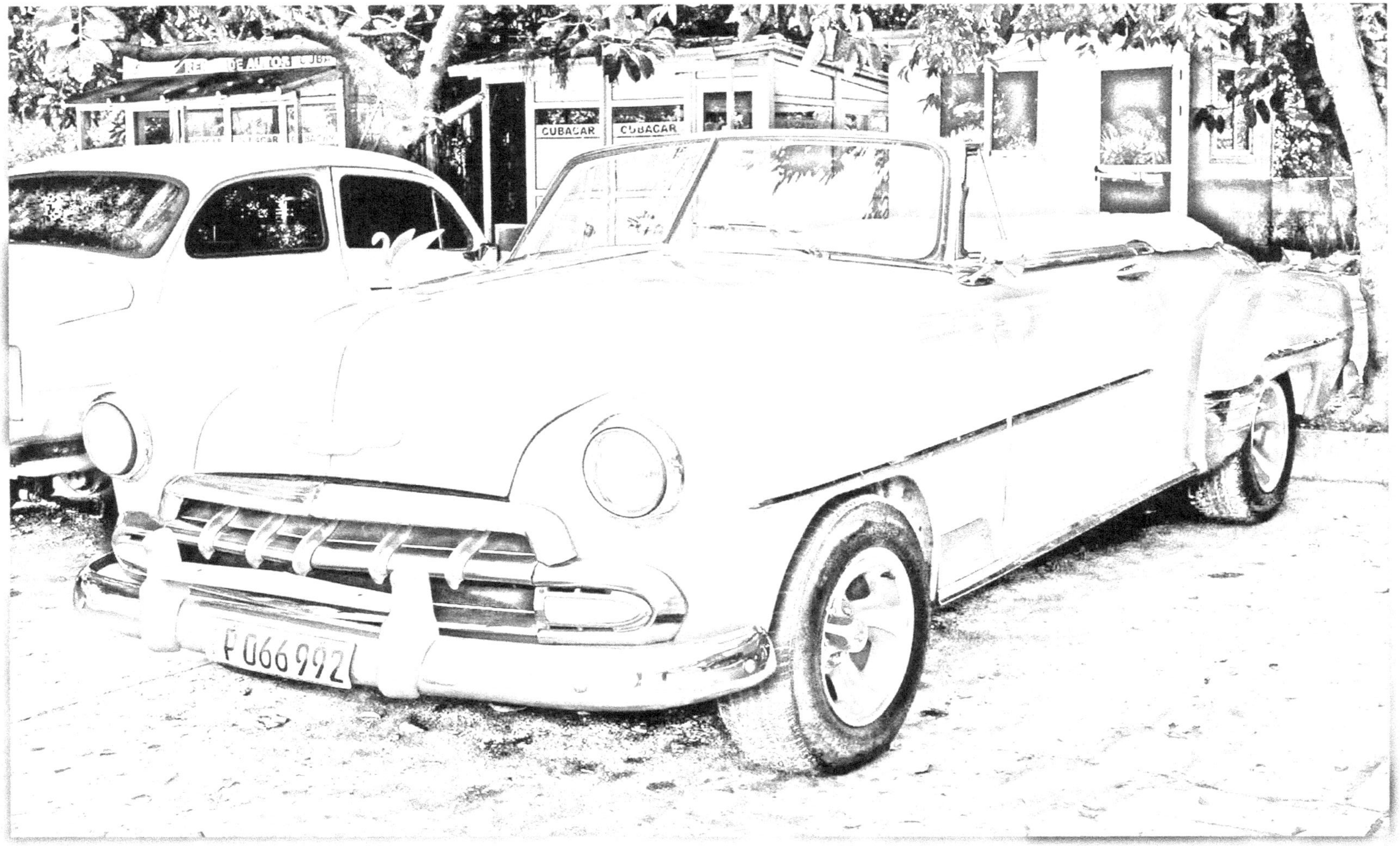
CUBACAR
CUBACAR
F 066992

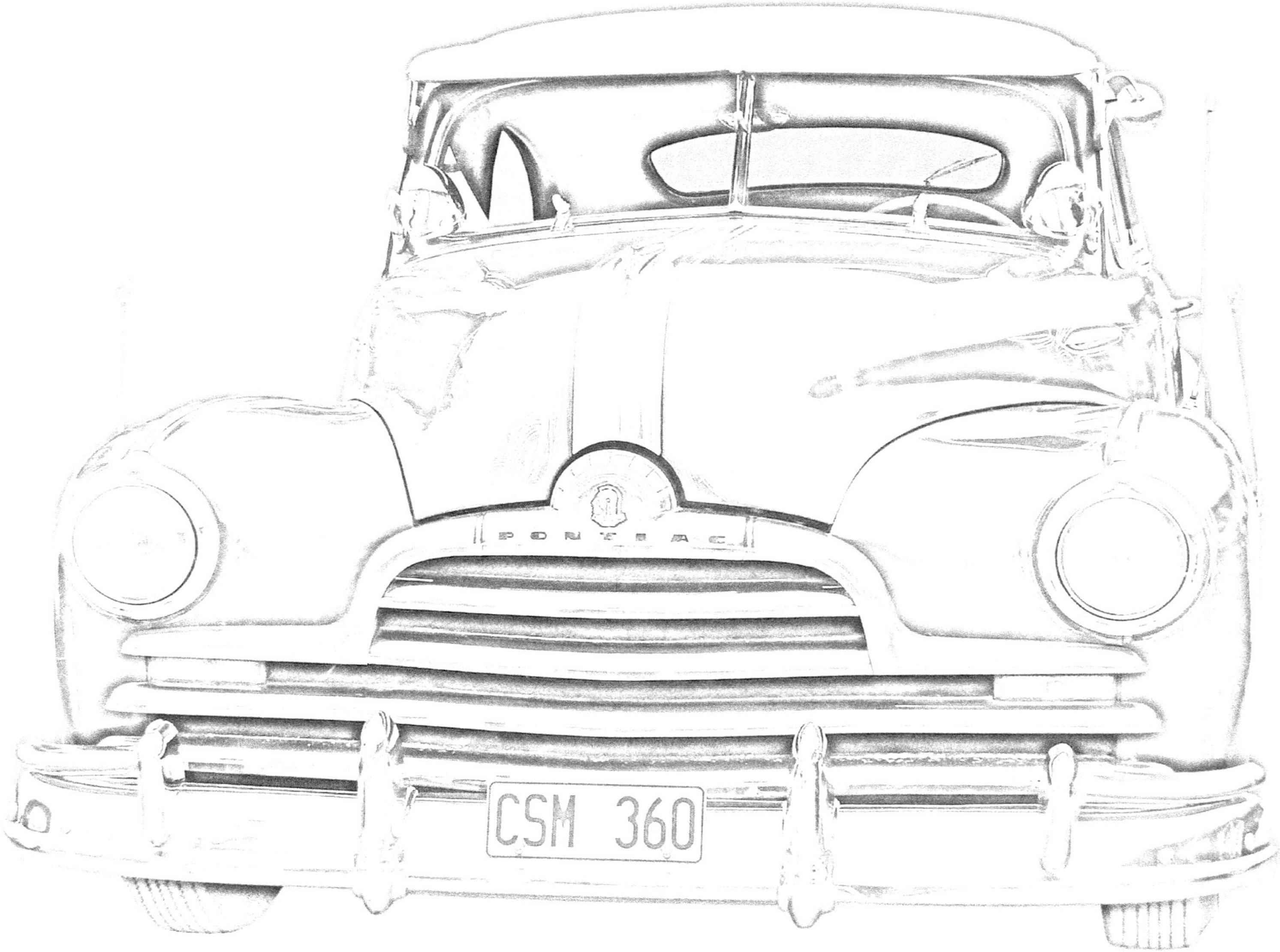
PONTIAC
CSM 360

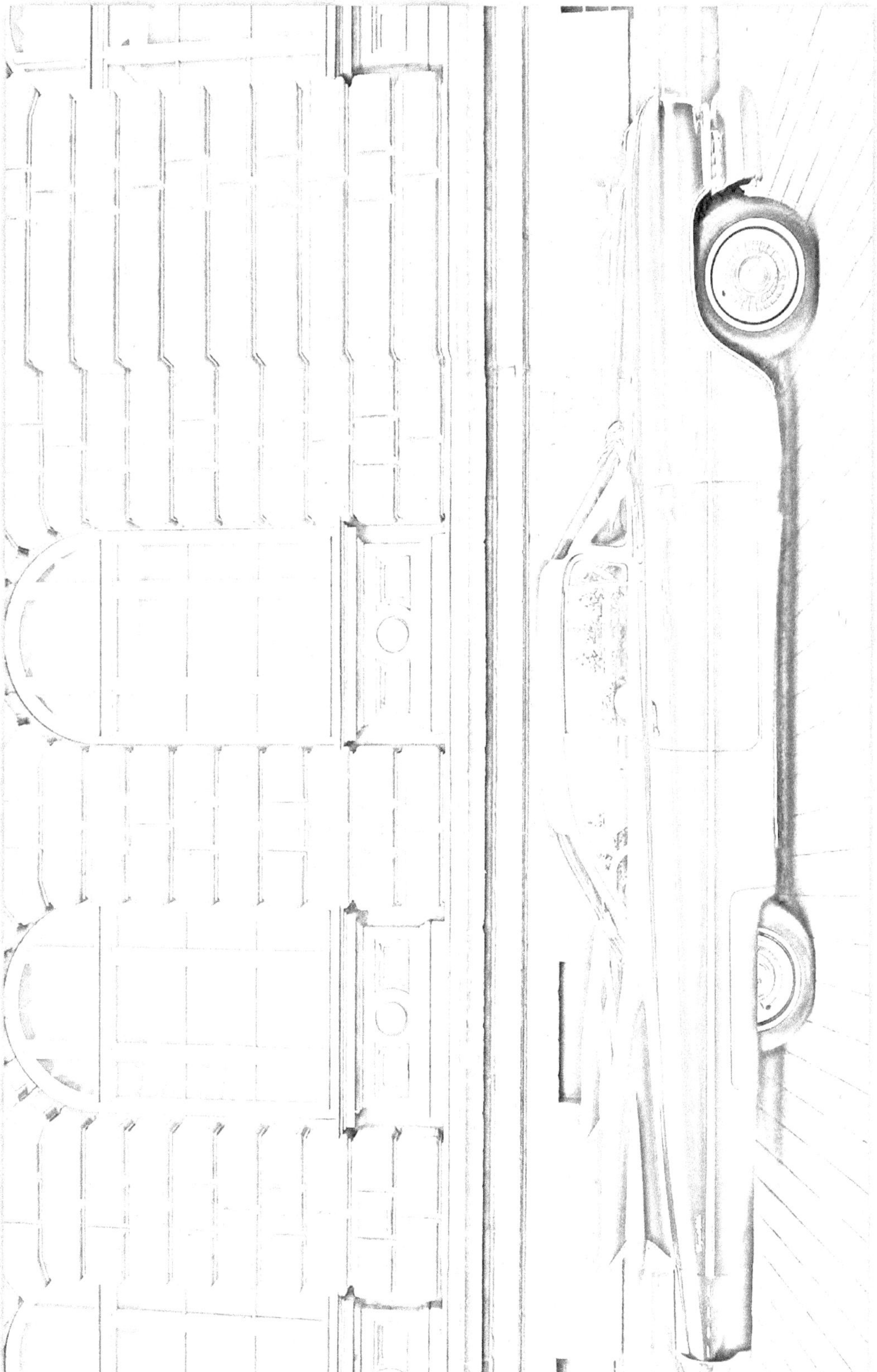

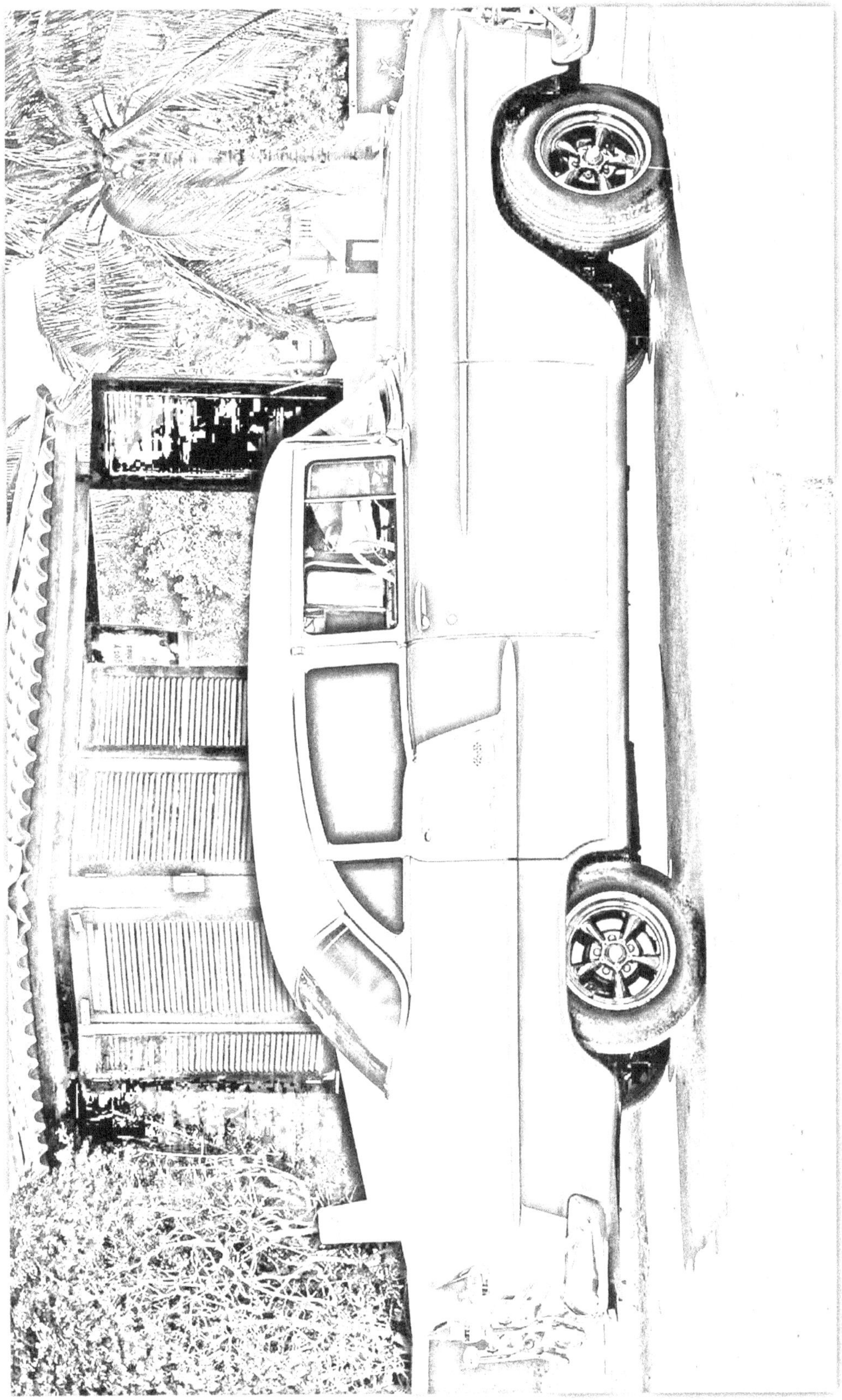

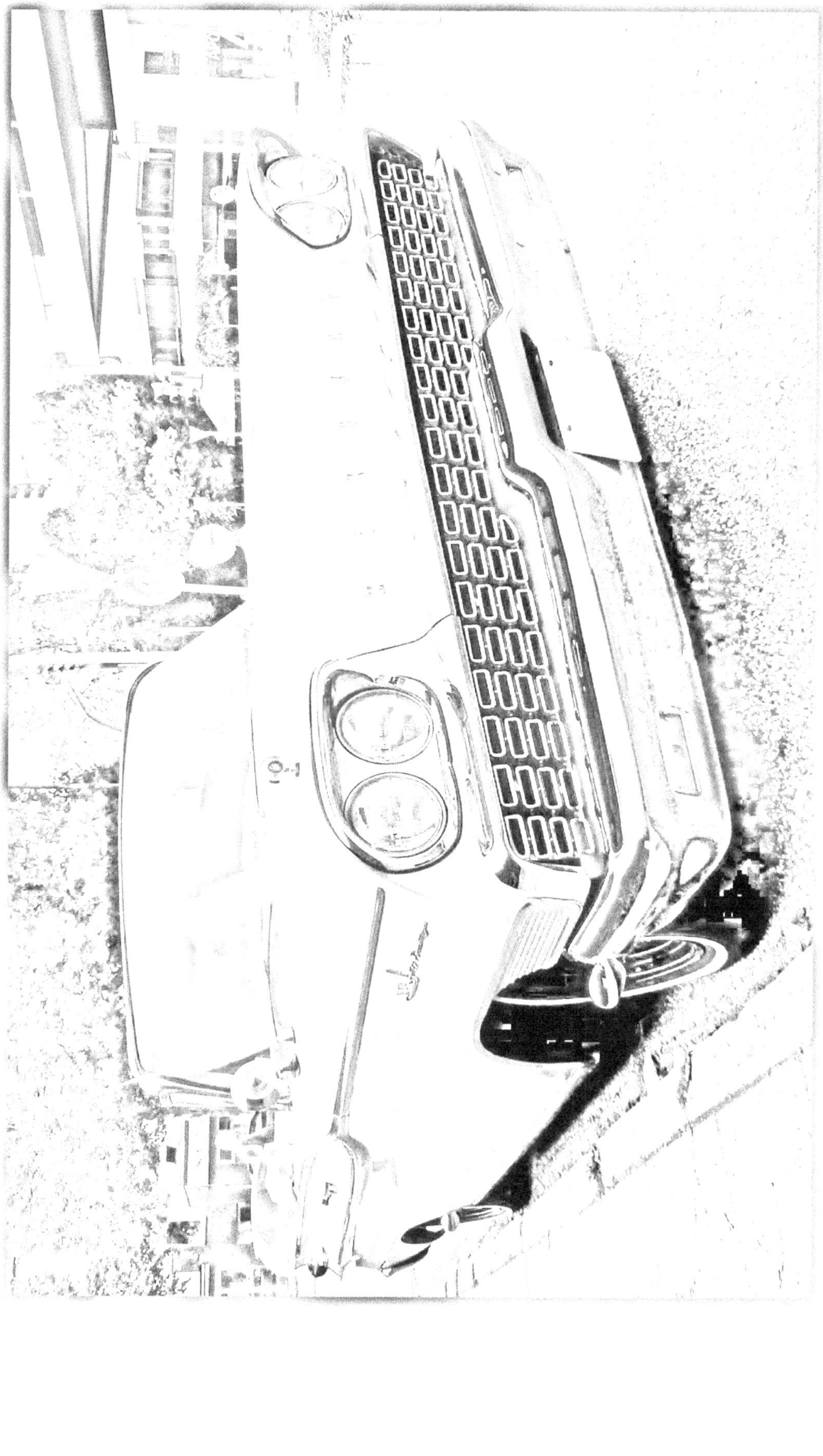

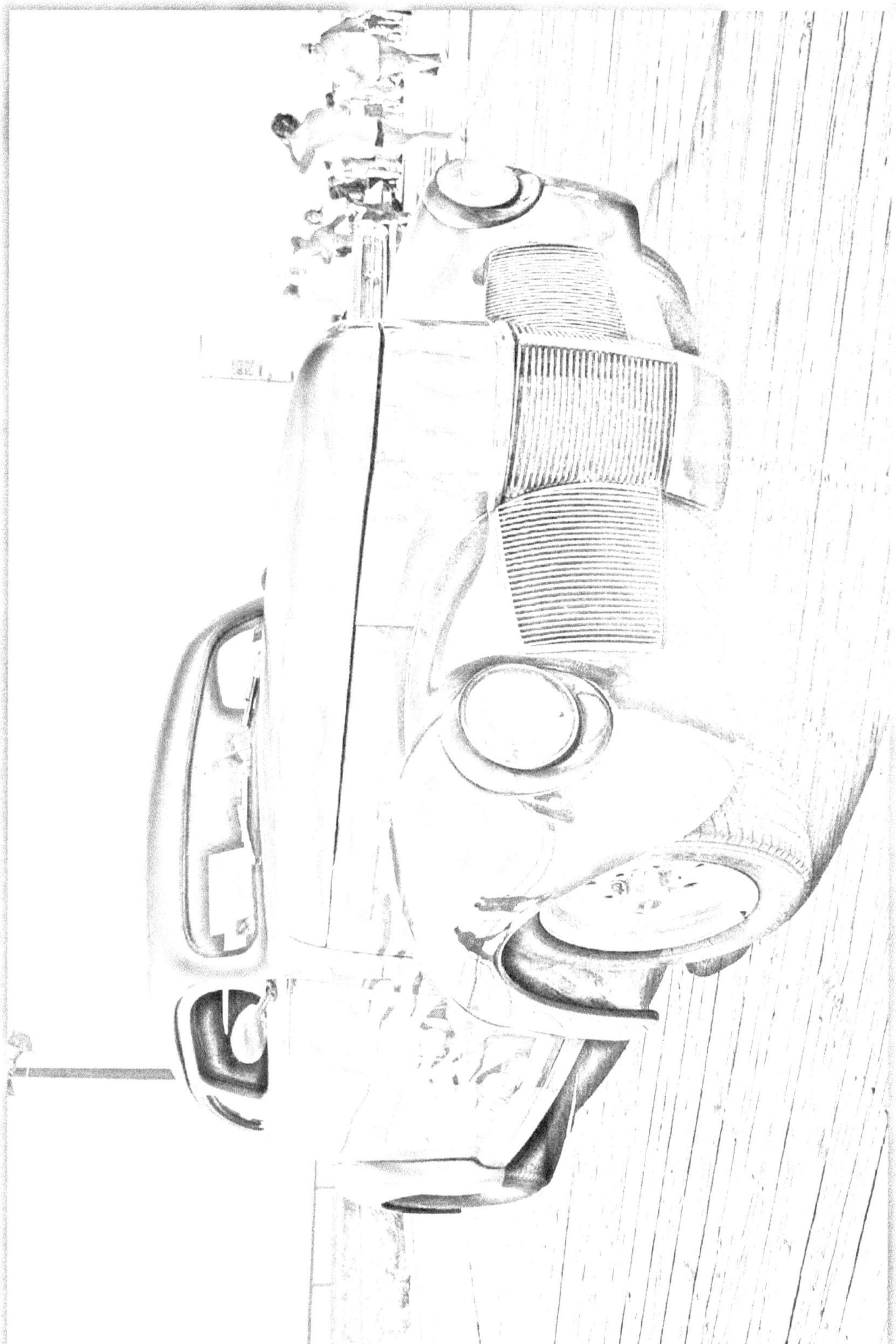

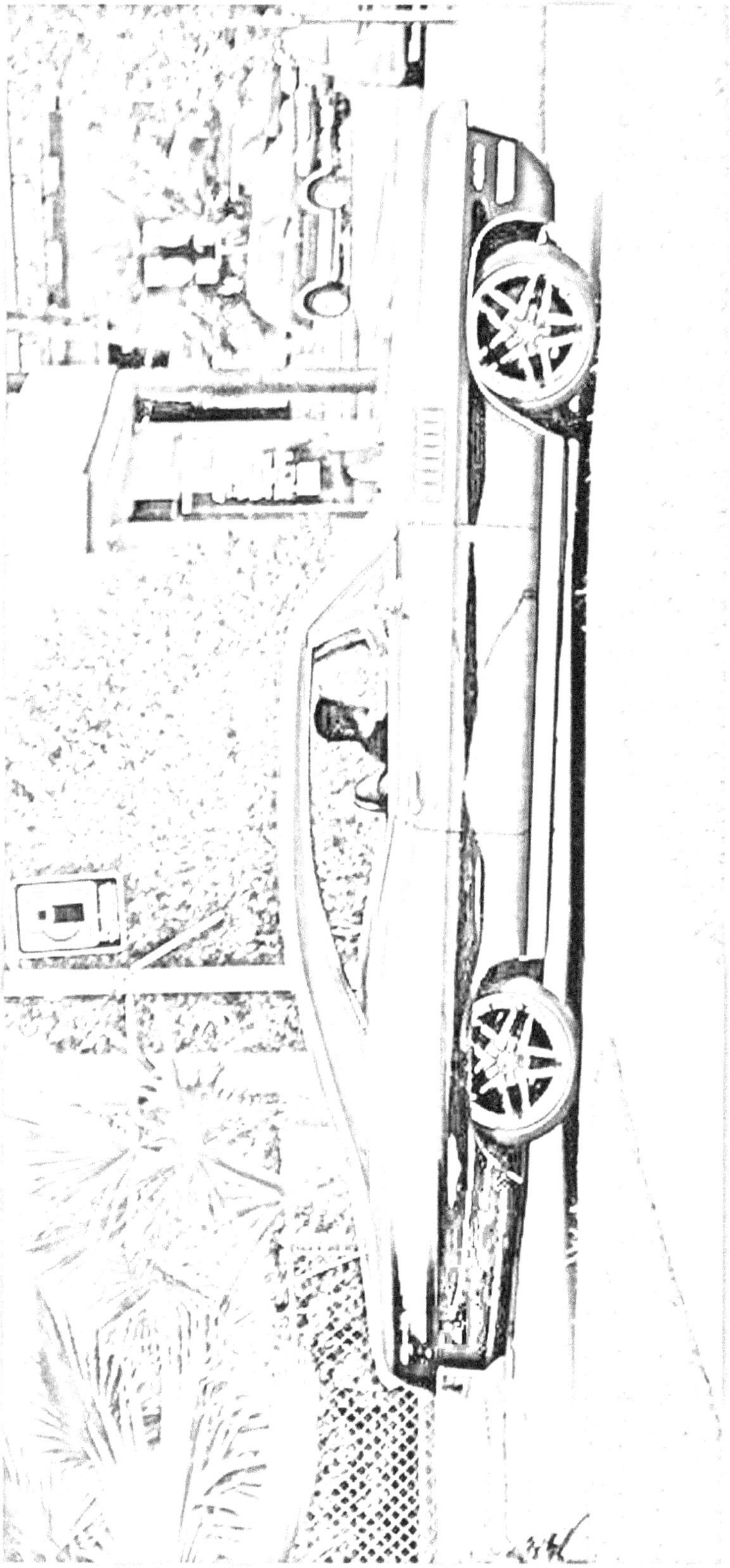

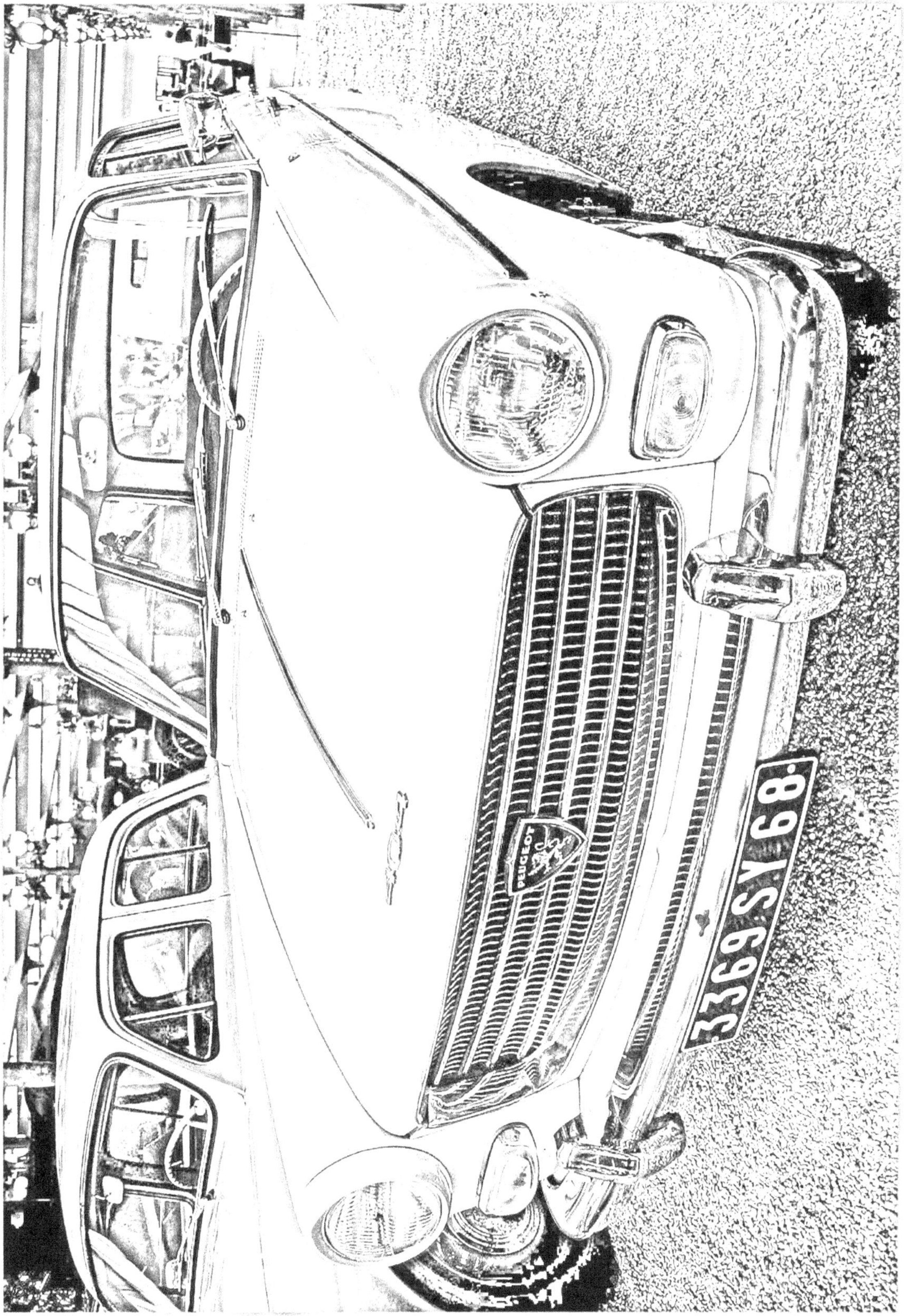
3369 SY 68
PEUGEOT

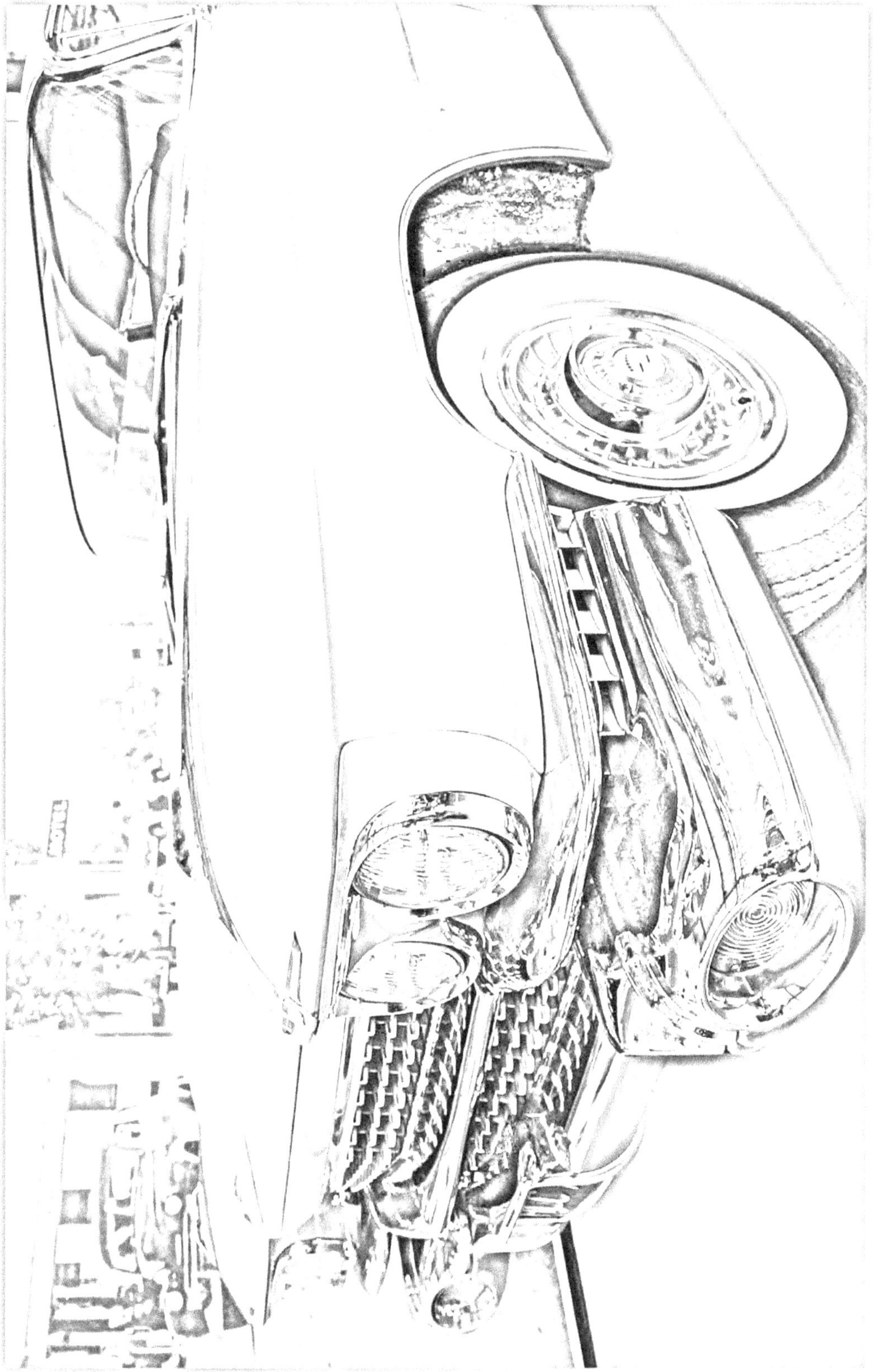

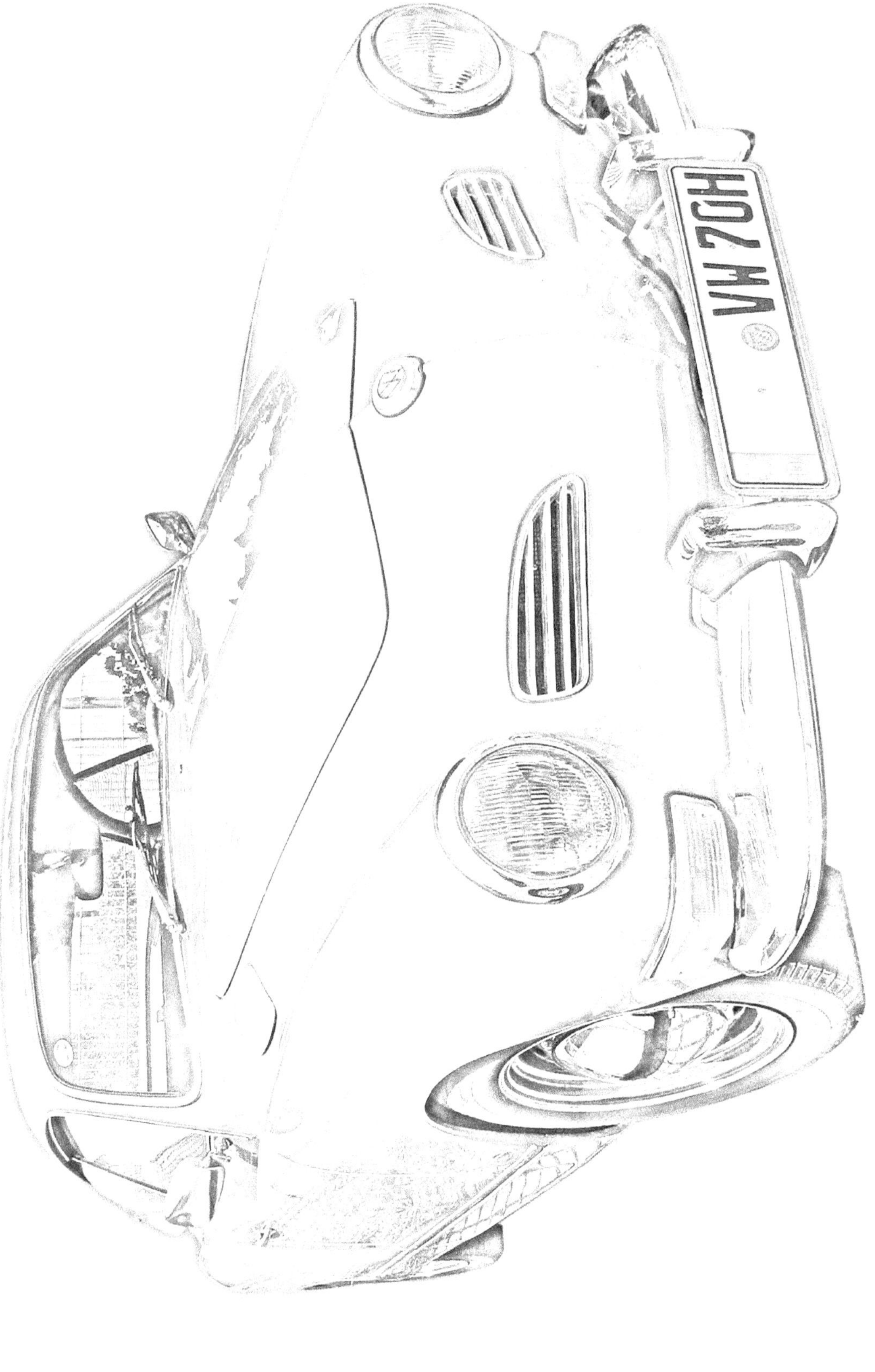

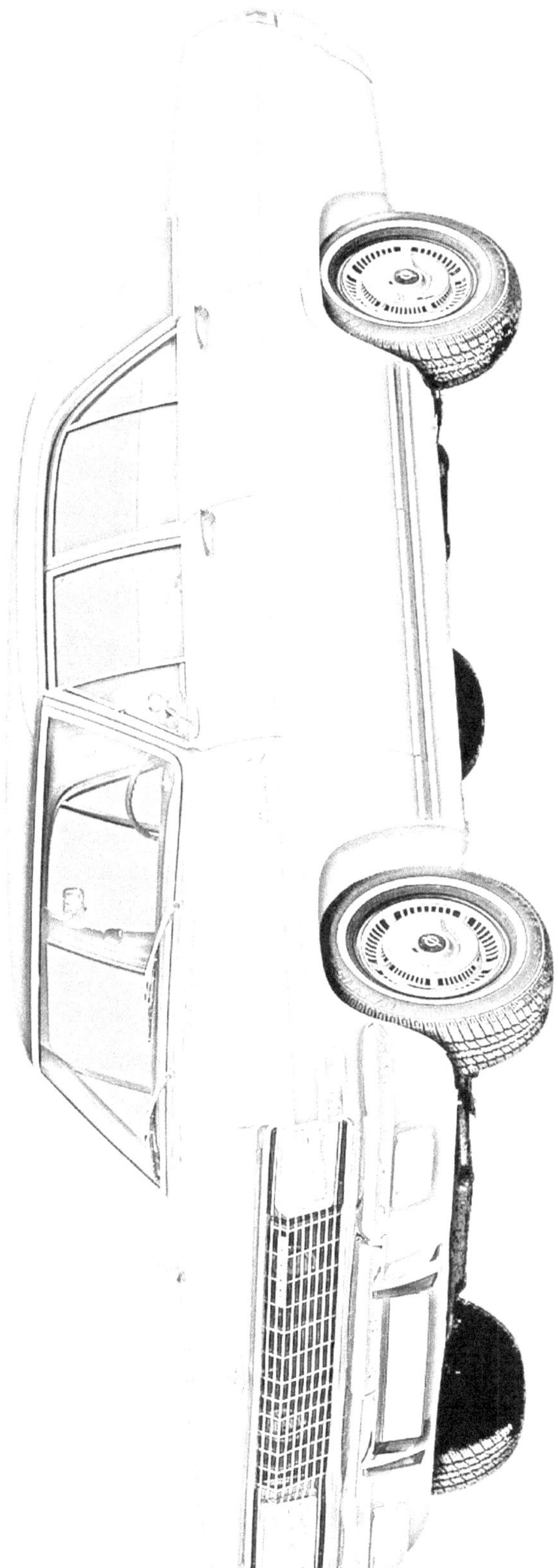

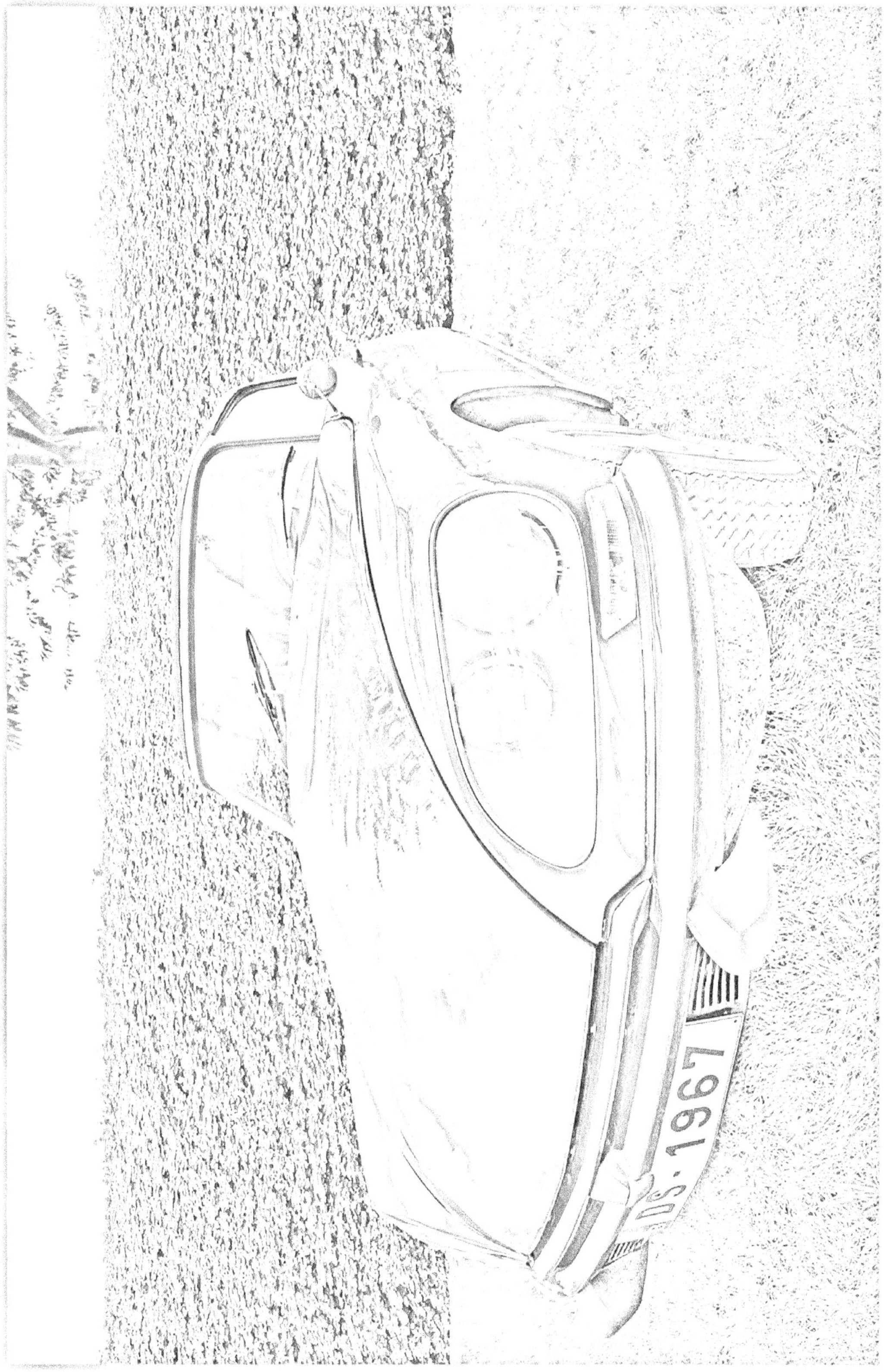
DS·1967

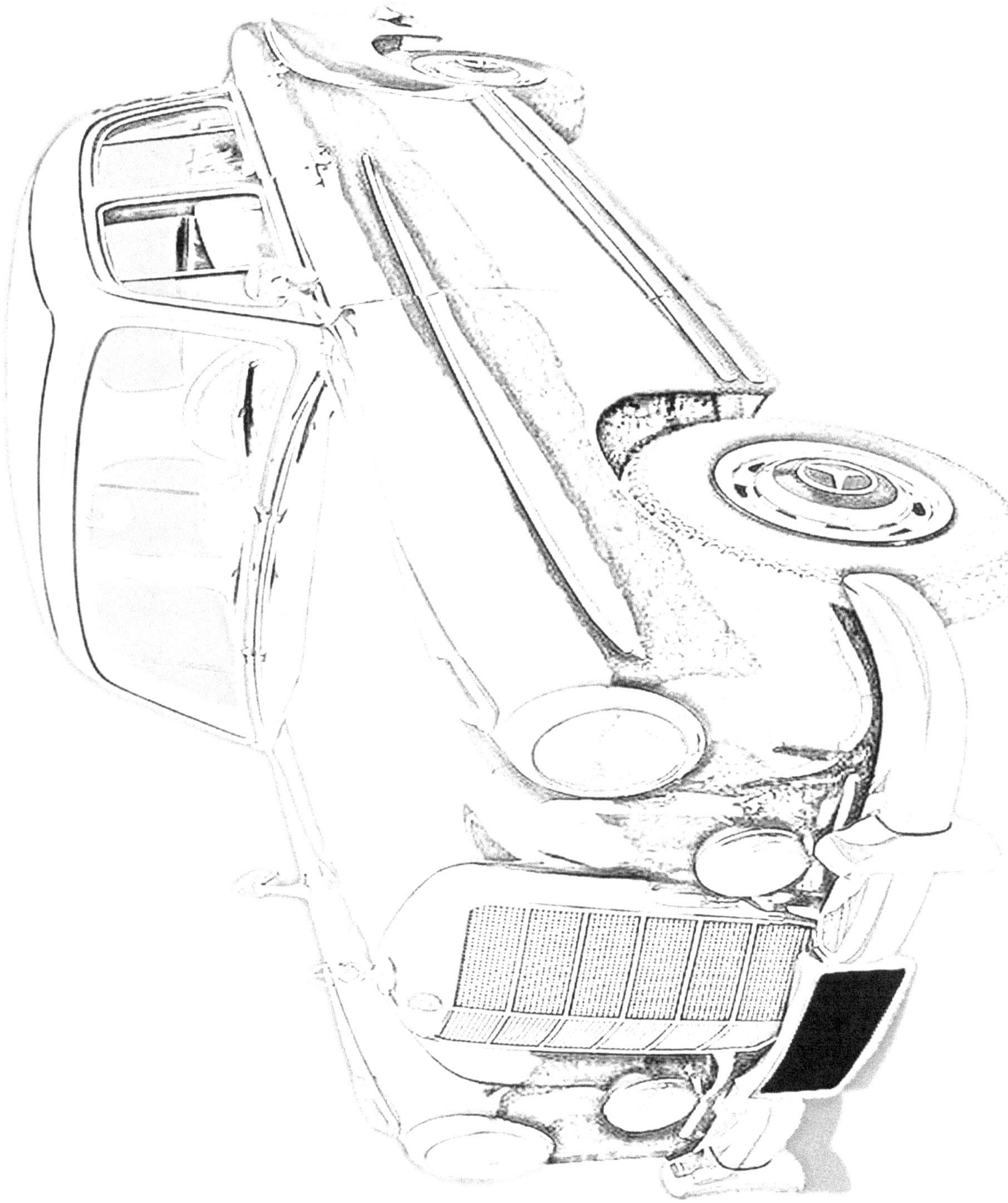

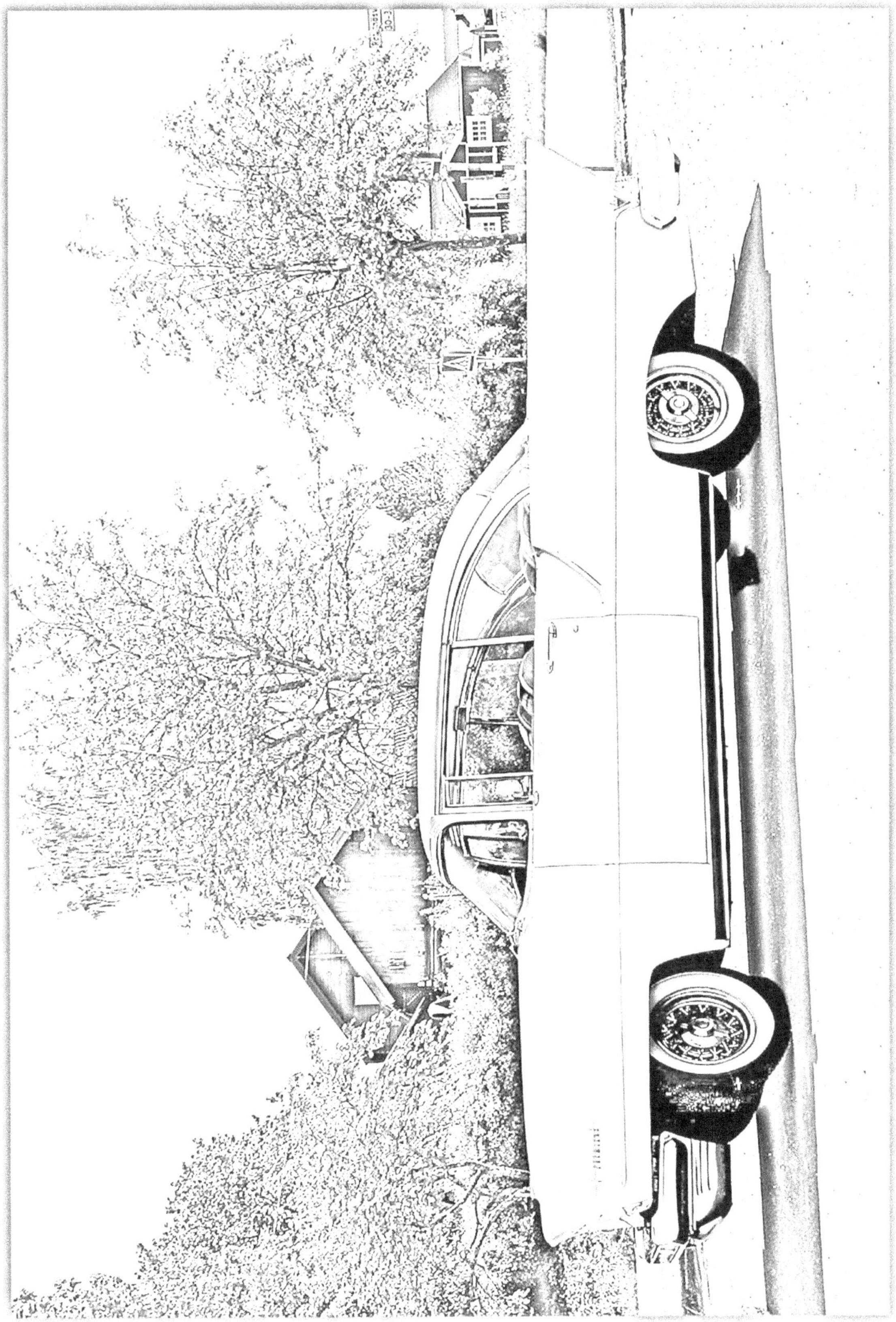

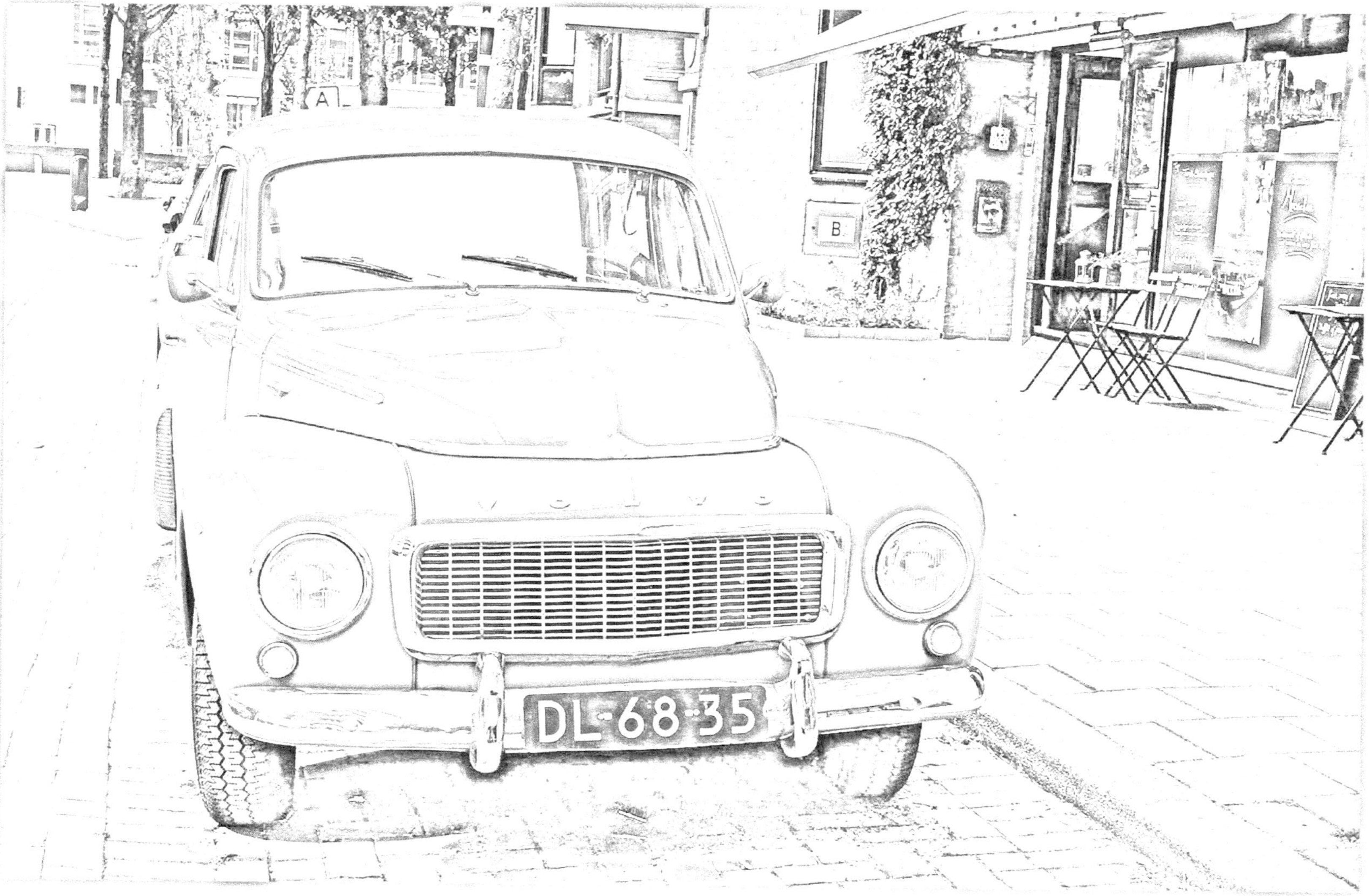
A
B
VOLVO
DL-68-35

www.ingramcontent.com/pod-product-compliance
Lightning Source LLC
Chambersburg PA
CBHW081730220526
45468CB00008B/2048
* 9 7 8 1 9 8 3 5 8 9 2 2 5 *